NEW DIRECTIONS FOR INSTITUTIONAL RESEARCH

J. Fredericks Volkwein, *Penn State University*
EDITOR-IN-CHIEF

Larry H. Litten, *Dartmouth College*
ASSOCIATE EDITOR

What Contributes to Job Satisfaction Among Faculty and Staff

Linda Serra Hagedorn
University of Southern California

EDITOR

Number 105, Spring 2000

JOSSEY-BASS PUBLISHERS
San Francisco

WHAT CONTRIBUTES TO JOB SATISFACTION AMONG FACULTY AND STAFF
Linda Serra Hagedorn (ed.)
New Directions for Institutional Research, no. 105
Volume XXVII, Number 1
J. Fredericks Volkwein, Editor-in-Chief

New Directions for Institutional Research is indexed in *College Student Personnel Abstracts, Contents Pages in Education,* and *Current Index to Journals in Education* (ERIC).

Microfilm copies of issues and chapters are available in 16mm and 35mm, as well as microfiche in 105mm, through University Microfilms Inc., 300 North Zeeb Road, Ann Arbor, Michigan 48106-1346.

ISSN 0271-0579   ISBN 0-7879-5438-1

NEW DIRECTIONS FOR INSTITUTIONAL RESEARCH is part of The Jossey-Bass Higher and Adult Education Series and is published quarterly by Jossey-Bass Inc., Publishers, 350 Sansome Street, San Francisco, California 94104-1342 (publication number USPS 098-830). Periodicals postage paid at San Francisco, California, and at additional mailing offices. POSTMASTER: Send address changes to New Directions for Institutional Research, Jossey-Bass Inc., Publishers, 350 Sansome Street, San Francisco, California 94104-1342.

SUBSCRIPTIONS cost $56.00 for individuals and $99.00 for institutions, agencies, and libraries.

EDITORIAL CORRESPONDENCE should be sent to J. Fredericks Volkwein, Center for the Study of Higher Education, Penn State University, 403 South Allen Street, Suite 104, University Park, PA 16801-5252.

Photograph of the library by Michael Graves at San Juan Capistrano by Chad Slattery © 1984. All rights reserved.

www.josseybass.com

Printed in the United States of America on acid-free recycled paper containing 100 percent recovered waste paper, of which at least 20 percent is postconsumer waste.

THE ASSOCIATION FOR INSTITUTIONAL RESEARCH was created in 1966 to bene-fit, assist, and advance research leading to improved understanding, planning, and operation of institutions of higher education. Publication policy is set by its Publications Committee.

PUBLICATIONS COMMITTEE

Richard A. Voorhees (Chair)	Colorado Community College and Occupational Education System
Craig Clagett	Prince Georges Community College
Eric L. Dey	University of Michigan
Jonathan Fife	George Washington University
Susan H. Frost	Emory University
Deborah Olsen	Indiana University

EX-OFFICIO MEMBERS OF THE PUBLICATIONS COMMITTEE

John C. Smart	Memphis State University, Department of Leadership
Richard Howard	Montana State University–Bozeman
J. Fredericks Volkwein	Penn State University
Mardy T. Eimers	University of Missouri
Dolores H. Vura	California State University–Fullerton
Jacquelyn L. Frost	Purdue University

For information about the Association for Institutional Research, write to the following address:

AIR Executive Office
114 Stone Building
Florida State University
Tallahassee, FL 32306-4462

(850) 644-4470

air@mailer.fsu.edu
http://airweb.org

CONTENTS

Editor's Notes

The chapters in this volume dissect and examine various members of the campus community to suggest the factors that will promote job satisfaction and thereby (indirectly) promote other positive outcomes. These notes will briefly comment on the practical side of the suggestions made in the chapters with reference to the conceptual framework of faculty job satisfaction presented as Figure 1.1 (see Chapter One). I have divided the essay into the two major segments of the model, namely, mediators and triggers (see Chapter One for definitions of all terms).

Mediators

A mediator is a variable or a situation that influences (moderates) outcomes and relationships between other variables or situations. The chapters in this volume agree on the importance and salience of mediators such as achievement, recognition, responsibility, and advancement. Certainly institutions have the power to promote these aspects of the job. Karen Bauer's practical suggestions (Chapter Eight) for classified employees may equally apply to faculty and administrators. She reminds us that recognition does not necessarily mean high institutional costs and suggests such rewards as premium parking spots, computer-related equipment, awards such as employee (faculty) of the month programs, and feature articles in the campus newspaper.

The use of the sabbatical (see Chapter Six by Celina Sima) to promote achievement and advancement is also a very doable approach to satisfaction and offers positive outcomes for the faculty who use the time productively for their development, colleagues who are challenged to new projects, and certainly the students who will benefit from the new knowledge.

Demographics. Most of the chapters cite gender as an important mediator to job satisfaction; additionally, many mention the role of ethnicity. However on the practical side, demographic divisions present problems to institutions. The option of separating individuals by demographics and then creating unique paths to achievement and recognition are neither practical nor equitable. Separate can never be equal. On the practical side is an honest examination of the factors that are discriminatory towards any particular group. The questions posed by Becky Ropers-Huilman (Chapter Two) can be adapted for any demographic group and are reasonable starting points to detect bias and frame an appropriate response.

The importance of discipline or department is made plain by the chapter on medical faculty (Chapter Three) and others. The role of faculty member may be similar regardless of discipline, but certainly there are marked differences between a professor of the fine arts and a professor of thoracic surgery; both differ from the community college instructor who teaches welding. One size does not fit all and factors pertaining to satisfaction must be considered within this arena.

Environment (Working Conditions). Few would argue that pleasant surroundings encourage satisfaction. Suggestions in the chapters include providing places where faculty, students, and staff can meet; updating equipment; providing day care; and sponsoring special events. Although these suggestions come with a financial price tag, the chapters in this volume argue that it will be money well spent.

Triggers

As the editor of this volume, I initially contacted the authors and requested their participation in the penning of a chapter. I communicated my clear expectations but attempted to encourage each author to write freely from his or her area of expertise. As I read through the initial drafts I was surprised at the number of chapters that reflected or included life satisfaction within the construct of job satisfaction. It appears that family, personal circumstances, mood, and other of life's affairs seemingly removed from the job are in reality permanently entrenched. Life satisfaction is not static, and in the course of its ebb and flow we encounter those triggers (significant life events) hypothesized in the model of Chapter One. Although life circumstances are very important to job satisfaction, this area offers less possibilities for effective intervention by the institution. Many colleges and universities recognize the intrusion by life circumstances and provide free or subsidized counseling services, health care and legal referrals, various support groups, job placement assistance for trailing spouses or partners, and discounts for sporting and other recreational events. These types of interventions are welcomed by workers and may assist them to work through life's problems (or life's joys). Despite brave (and undoubtedly costly) efforts by the institution, triggers (such as divorce, death of a loved one, birth, and so on) will pull faculty and staff attention away from the job. Perhaps compassion is what is most doable. Extending tenure clocks, parental leave, and provisions for personal time are examples that may help good employees work through temporary conditions.

Conclusion

The volume authors have combed the literature, tested the models, and presented their synthesis. After you read the chapters of this volume, I suggest that you return to the conceptual framework of Figure 1.1 and contemplate the utility of the model. Does the model offer a framework for studying job satisfaction? What does the model lack? What is superfluous? How should it be modified? Finally, I ask you to contemplate what factors (positive or negative) would propel you on the job satisfaction continuum. All of the chapters agree that job satisfaction is complex and misunderstood. I would like to recruit your help in sorting the practical from the ideal. Together let us focus on the goal of improving and honing a model that will be of great utility to institutional researchers, administrators, faculty, and others who recognize the importance of faculty and staff satisfaction. I look forward to receiving your responses at <Lsh@usc.edu>.

Linda Serra Hagedorn
Editor

LINDA SERRA HAGEDORN is associate professor of higher education and senior research associate at the Center for Higher Education Policy Analysis at the University of Southern California. She is also chair of the Community College Leadership program.

1

An introduction and framework for the volume, this chapter introduces a general model of faculty satisfaction, applies it to college and university faculty, and tests it using a national database.

Conceptualizing Faculty Job Satisfaction: Components, Theories, and Outcomes

Linda Serra Hagedorn

> The well being of the university depends on its ability to recruit and retain a talented professoriat. Our national well being depends on our ability to develop a happy, emotionally healthy, and productive next generation.
> —Nancy Hensel (1991, p. 79)

Although the importance of faculty satisfaction is readily apparent to college professors, it may appear truly different to outsiders of the ivory tower. To the casual observer, faculty satisfaction is at best a trivial concern easily superseded by the more urgent concerns of student outcomes such as academic achievement and financial efficiency. Whether or not Hensel (1991) overstated the importance of faculty satisfaction in the opening quote by linking it with our national well-being, popular opinion has been coaxed to distrust the college professor and pay scant attention to faculty satisfaction. As early as the 1930s criticisms of the academic system were surfacing (Hutchins, 1936). The tone of criticism changed through the decades. Consider Holland's (1985) portrayal of academe in the 1960s and early 1970s as a bleak episode in the history of American higher education. The 1980s brought Bloom's popular book *The Closing of the American Mind* (1987), casting a dark shadow over the American higher education system and fomenting considerable public criticism. More recently, we witness the harsh treatment of the education community in general through popular books like *Profscam* (Sykes, 1988), *Inside American Education: The Decline, the Deception, the Dogmas* (Sowell, 1993), and *Tenured Radicals: How Politics has Corrupted Higher Education* (Kimball, 1990). As we enter the twenty-first century, criticizing college professors looms like a contemporary sport without shortage of participants or spectators. Television, radio, and newspapers cast college professors as content, lazy, and arrogant. Academic jobs are depicted as low-pressured, complete with short working hours, high salaries, and lifetime job security.

This volume recasts the academic profession and debunks popular views. Its mission is to paint a realistic portrait of the college professional and to argue that the study of faculty (and staff) satisfaction is warranted, appropriate, and needed. College professors typically work in environments that are high-pressured, multifaceted, and without clear borders. Stress abounds. Moreover, the volume establishes that positive college environments produce important positive outcomes for all players, including students.

The present chapter is divided into three major sections. The first, dealing with the psychology of job satisfaction, introduces a general framework. The second section applies the framework specifically to college and university faculty. Finally, the third section looks at actual outcomes of job satisfaction using a national database of faculty.

The Psychology of Job Satisfaction

Although job satisfaction is a topic of interest for business in general and labor relations in particular, it is truly surprising that so few theoretical models exist to try to explain, predict, or understand it. Further, the extant literature rests heavily on old models that at minimum are in dire need of rejuvenation and modification. With these caveats firmly in place, there is general agreement that the concept of job satisfaction is complex and convoluted. In truth, no single conceptual model can completely and accurately portray the construct. Nevertheless, I offer Figure 1.1, Conceptual Framework of Faculty Job Satisfaction, as a strategy to sort and categorize the factors that compose and contribute to job satisfaction. Basically, the model hypothesizes two types of constructs that interact and affect job satisfaction—triggers and mediators.

I define a *trigger* as a significant life event that may be either related or unrelated to the job. Several psychological studies have indicated that major life events or triggers result in a change in reference, a change in self, as well as a change in work-related responses (Latack, 1984; Waskel and Owens, 1991). The other type of construct, a *mediator,* can technically be described as a variable or situation that influences (moderates) the relationships between other variables or situations producing an interaction effect. The hypothesized mediating variables represent situations, developments, and extenuating circumstances that provide the context in which job satisfaction must be considered. Mediators signify the complexity of satisfaction—there is no "one size fits all at all times" nor can a list of factors that always encourage positive outlooks on the job be developed. The curved arrow of Figure 1.1 signifies the complex feedback between the state of mediators and the triggers that further affect the nature of satisfaction.

The conceptual model contains six unique triggers: (1) change in life stage, (2) change in family-related or personal circumstances (for example, birth, death, divorce, illness of self or significant other), (3) change in rank or tenure, (4) transfer to a new institution, (5) change in perceived justice, and (6) change in mood or emotional state. The effect of triggers will be examined in detail in the next section of the chapter.

The model includes three types of mediators: (1) motivators and hygienes, (2) demographics, and (3) environmental conditions. The mediators and triggers form an elementary structure and framework in which faculty job satisfaction may be examined.

Motivators and Hygienes. The existence of motivators and hygienes is based on a predominant and influential theory of job satisfaction developed in the late 1950s and early 1960s by Frederick Herzberg and his colleagues (Herzberg, Mausner, Peterson, and Capwell, 1957; Herzberg,

Figure 1.1. Conceptual Framework of Faculty Job Satisfaction

Mediators			Triggers
Motivators and Hygienes	Demographics	Environmental Conditions	Change or Transfer
Achievement	Gender	Collegial	Change in life stage
Recognition	Ethnicity	relationships	Change in family-related or
Work itself	Institutional	Student quality	personal circumstances
Responsibility	type	or relationships	Change in rank or tenure
Advancement	Academic	Administration	Transfer to new institution
Salary	discipline	Institutional	Change in perceived justice
		climate or	Change in mood or emo-
		culture	tional state

Job Satisfaction Continuum

Disengagement   Acceptance/tolerance   Appreciation of job
                                                      Actively engaged in work

Mausner, and Snyderman, 1959). The theory promotes the existence of factors labeled *motivators* which work to increase satisfaction while other factors labeled *hygienes* decrease dissatisfaction or result in de-motivation. Although Herzberg's theories were developed about forty years ago, his work continues to be recognized and his contribution praised (Wren and Greenwood, 1998). Herzberg's research (1959) identified fourteen first-level job factors related with job satisfaction and dissatisfaction: achievement, recognition, the work itself, responsibility, possibility of advancement, possibility of growth, salary status, the quality of interpersonal relations with superiors, the quality of interpersonal relations with peers, technical supervision, agreement with company policies and administration, pleasant working conditions, external factors from personal life, and job security. But Herzberg ultimately found only achievement, recognition, work itself, responsibility, advancement, and (to a lesser degree) salary to be influential in either increasing job satisfaction or decreasing job dissatisfaction. Herzberg believed that the causes of satisfaction and dissatisfaction were distinct and hence the theory has been labeled the two-factor theory of job satisfaction. Recent and more exacting studies have verified much of Herzberg's work (Diener, 1985; Gallagher and Einhorn, 1976; Gawel, 1997; Knight and Westbrook, 1999). Interpreting Herzberg's factors indicates that the intensity of the work and the level of involvement achieved by the worker moderate job satisfaction. Thus, when a worker feels a high level of achievement, is intensely involved, and is appropriately compensated by recognition, responsibility, and salary, job satisfaction is enhanced and job dissatisfaction is decreased.

Ample evidence in the literature supports the important role of the second group of mediators, demographics, in job satisfaction (Bullers, 1999; Hagedorn, 1994; Hagedorn, 1996; Hagedorn and Sax, 1999; Olsen, Maple, and Stage, 1995; Smart, 1990). Demographics, unlike the other hypothesized mediators, are stable and remain fixed throughout the career. Gender is the most researched demographic; yet the evidence remains mixed with respect to its specific interactions with job satisfaction. However, there is considerable agreement that males are more satisfied with their salary and benefits (Hemmasi, Graf, and Lust, 1992; Kelly, 1989); that family factors play a larger role for women (Bullers, 1999; Hagedorn and Sax, 1999); and that external factors such as the presence of discrimination or stereotyping frequently interacts with the job satisfaction of female employees (Jena, 1999).

The evidence on the interplay of ethnicity and job satisfaction is in constant flux. But in general, the literature indicates that minority workers are likely to meet with race-related stressors (Holder and Vaux, 1998). The nature and extent of the stressors is complex and depends on numerous factors such as the racial composition of surrounding staff—both coworkers and supervisors (Kirby and Jackson, 1999) as well as *situational salience,* the level of distinctiveness and interpretation of token status experienced by the worker (Niemann and Dovidio, 1998). Thus, the demographic mediators of gender and ethnicity may function to pull faculty members away from academic pursuits and create interference with the job.

The last two demographics, institutional type and academic discipline, are specific to college professors but represent important categories that affect the nature of job satisfaction. Like gender and ethnicity, these factors create in-groups of workers who share certain similar characteristics and interests and out-groups of workers whose responsibilities and job requirements are defined somewhat differently. The difference between the disciplines themselves, as well as the jobs of professors who research and teach them, has long been studied in the higher education literature. As a result, several schemes have been devised to try to make sense of the differences and are almost always used in higher education research studies (Biglan, 1973a, 1973b; Stark, 1998).

The third group of mediators, labeled *environmental*, encompasses working conditions including the social and working relationships established with administrators (bosses), colleagues (coworkers), and students (subordinates). Of all of the mediators, those in the environmental domain are the most likely to be transitory and subject to change. In short, the labor relations and organizational theory research indicates that positive social and working relationships as well as satisfying working conditions are conducive to increased levels of job-related satisfaction (Carnevale and Rios, 1995).

Although there is ample support for the inclusion of stress in any model referring to job satisfaction, its absence from the conceptual framework was not an oversight. Rather, stress is perceived as an all-inclusive term that overlaps with virtually all aspects of the job. The model places stress not as a primary indicator but rather as a consequence of negative responses to the mediators and triggers.

Response of Job Satisfaction. The final portion of the model is the actual product, evidence, and the result of job satisfaction. Although no appropriate metric capable of precisely categorizing or gauging levels of job satisfaction exists, any worker can attest that its presence can be felt and its consequences observed. Figure 1.1 incorporates worker response as a criterion for job satisfaction. Like most of life's expressions and emotional responses, job satisfaction is better represented by a continuum than by discrete categories. However, for purposes of conceptualization, I have identified three points on the continuum and have supplied the labels of (1) appreciation, (2) acceptance or tolerance, and (3) disengagement. Thus, a worker who is experiencing a high level of job satisfaction would be likely to appreciate his or her position and be proud of the organization, resulting in a high likelihood of job engagement and productivity. On the other side of the continuum is the disengaged worker who, due to very low levels of satisfaction, is not actively engaged in the work, does not feel any affinity with the organization, and finally is not excited or desirous to contribute to the benefit of the institution. Between the two extremes lie the majority of workers who have accepted and evolved with their work-related roles. The theory developed in this chapter is that the effects of the mediators and triggers play a large role in determining a faculty member's satisfaction level as gauged on the continuum.

The Framework Applied to College and University Faculty

This section will focus more specifically on college professors by concentrating on the triggers identified in the framework.

Life Stages. The prominent psychosocial work of Erickson, Levinson, Sheehy, and Neugarten indicates the presence of a social clock triggering predictable stages in adult development. For example, Levinson's (1978, 1996) theory promotes cycles of major transitory periods followed by periods of stability with consequences that affect most aspects of life. Because life and work are intertwined, the transition into life stages plays a prominent role in job-related outcomes. Several researchers have explored the overlap between life stages and job stages specifically for college faculty. For example, Baldwin (1979) proposed a tri-stage theory of the faculty career consisting of (1) early career, (2) midcareer, and (3) late career. I later validated a model of faculty career stages based on reported years until retirement and tested a structural model to determine the unique contributors to job satisfaction for each group. Although low stress levels predicted satisfaction for the entire sample, differences by group membership did surface. Faculty with twenty-five years or more until reported retirement (labeled *novices*) derived satisfaction from the positive relationships with administration and interactions with students. For faculty who were between fifteen and twenty years from reported retirement (labeled *midcareerists*), satisfaction was strongly related to appropriate compensation. Finally, for those anticipating retirement in five years or less (labeled *disengagers*), job satisfaction was best predicted through positive relationships with administration as well as appropriate compensation (Hagedorn, 1994).

Both the career and life cycle theories predict a cycle change at midcareer and again at late career (triggers) causing faculty to enter a time when they realize life changes and feel the need for reexamination. The midcareer trigger can be likened to a midlife crisis in which earlier career doubts may resurface and faculty may ask self-directed questions such as: Is this what I want to do for the rest of my working life? Are my research and teaching meaningful? Have I made a difference? Am I a success? Similarly, new doubts and questions may arise again as faculty contemplate life after retirement. The questions during this second trigger may include: Now what? What can I do now that will best prepare me for the life I have left? How should I continue professional relationships? The life and career stage changes force faculty to redefine their perceptions of the job satisfaction mediators and thus result in movement on the job satisfaction continuum.

Change in Family-Related or Personal Circumstances. The birth of a baby, the death of someone close, marriage, divorce, illness, or another significant event occurring to oneself or to a significant other changes a faculty member's outlook on both life and the job. Researchers in the area of work-family conflict have found that conflict between the job and family concerns provide stress that ultimately can affect both psychological and physical health (Adams, King, and King, 1996). This trigger is highly interactive with gender as the conflict is generally more acute for females (Duxbury, Higgins, and Lee, 1994). Regardless of demographics, however, most of the mediators change in importance and role when a change in family-related circumstances occurs resulting in movement up or down the job satisfaction continuum.

Change in Rank or Tenure. Baldwin wrote "Professors change as they progress through the faculty ranks and as their careers place different demands on them" (1990, p. 20). A change in rank brings a new outlook on the position, different expectations, and a change in responsibility. Braskamp and Ory (1984) looked at the repercussions of rank through standardized interviews with forty-eight professors of different ranks. Their data supported the hypothesis that a promotion in rank can be likened to a progression to a different stage of development. More specifically, they found that assistant professors dwell on advancing in the profession; at the associate level the focus switches to the establishment of balance within professional life; and finally, full professors can define their professional life and fulfill their lifetime goals. Thus a promotion may trigger a change in sources of satisfaction. In support of the model, others have also found rank and tenure to be a powerful variable in the satisfaction of faculty (Tack and Patitu, 1992). Promotions or accrual of tenure alter the focus, the concerns, and subsequent goals, thus changing the mix of mediators and resulting in movement on the continuum.

Transfer to a Different Institution. Faculty tend to be quite mobile. Getting a firm idea of the magnitude of faculty turnover on a national basis is virtually impossible as the National Center for Education Statistics does not keep records of faculty mobility. However Harrigan (1999) quantified this movement as follows: "If all faculty were hired and retained until retirement after thirty years of service, we would expect an equilibrium turnover rate of about one-third of the faculty every ten years or 3.3 percent per year. An alternative hypothetical university, which hired all [of] its faculty on probation and which denied tenure to all of them in their seventh year, would have an equilibrium turnover rate of one-seventh or 14.3 percent per year. Thus, we would expect the 'normal' turnover rate to fall somewhere between these two extremes" (p. 1). Single-institution studies usually report migration levels consistent with Harrigan's estimates. Despite the dearth of information on faculty migration, it is an unwritten but well-known truism among faculty that the fastest and most direct path to a promotion in rank or a substantial raise in pay may be an offer from another institution. Regardless of the reasons why a faculty member moves to a different institution, the change in locale will always mean new surroundings, responsibilities, students, colleagues, and fitting oneself within a different institutional mission. Thus, like the other triggers, a change in institutions results in movement on the continuum.

Change in Perceived Justice. In two related studies of female college faculty (Hagedorn, 1996, 1998), I found a highly significant relationship between gender-based wage differentials and multiple measures of satisfaction. Job satisfaction and intent to remain in academe were more strongly related to gender-equitable salary structures than to level of salary. In other words, more dissatisfaction occurred when female faculty members perceived their salary as being less than that of their comparable male colleagues than when they felt that all faculty (regardless of gender) were underpaid. Equity regarding salary levels is, of course, only one example where perceived fairness may be a strong predictor of satisfaction. Other areas where discernment of justice or equity may play a role include practices of promotion, hiring, awarding of tenure, and nomination for awards. A sudden realization of inequity serves as a strong trigger and likely introduces a strong reaction followed by a significant move on the satisfaction continuum.

Change in Mood or Emotional State. The final trigger relates to affective disposition, such as mood or proclivity towards a fixed emotional state. Although complex and misunderstood, emotions play a vital role in all personal and social endeavors enveloping working attitudes (Izard, Kagan, and Zajonc, 1984; Young, 1996). While there may be little the institution can do to alter mood or disposition, a recent study of job applicants found that as much as 20 to 30 percent of the variance in work performance and attitudes was a direct result of preexisting personality factors (Furnham, Forde, and Ferrari, 1999). Supporting this finding is another recent inquiry that reported a high level of association between job satisfaction and mood (Weiss, Nicholas, and Daus, 1999). Thus, mood is a pivotal variable that is strongly responsible for one's location on the job satisfaction continuum.

Establishing Validity for the Model

The final section of this chapter will briefly address the validity of the model proposed in Figure 1.1. A forthcoming research article will fully explain the validation of the model; however, this chapter will provide a brief summary of the validation using the 1993 National Study of Postsecondary Faculty (NSOPF 1993), a large nationally representative database compiled by the National Center for Education Statistics (1993). Indicators and proxies for all of the model components were derived except for measures of collegial relationships and change in mood or emotional state. Table 1.1 provides information regarding the items and measures used for the mediators as well as for the measure of faculty job satisfaction; Table 1.2 provides similar

Table 1.1. Mediators from the NSOPF 1993 as Applied to the Conceptual Framework of Faculty Job Satisfaction

Motivators and Hygienes

Achievement	Number of publications and presentations
Recognition	Measures indicating chairperson status and engagement in funded or creative endeavors
Work itself	A derived measure comparing the actual proportions of time spent in research and teaching to the desired time spent in these activities
Responsibility	Number of committees served and chaired
Advancement	Derived measure calculated from time in rank
Salary	Natural log of salary

Demographics

Gender	Dichotomous variable indicating male or female
Ethnicity	Two dichotomous variables indicating if African American or Hispanic
Institutional type	Carnegie designation
Academic discipline	Categorized by Biglan type (hard/soft, pure/applied, life/nonlife)

Environmental Conditions

Collegial relationships	Item(s) measuring collegial relationships not available in the data set
Student quality or relationships	Satisfaction with student quality
Administration	Measure of satisfaction with administrative decisions
Institutional climate or culture	Measures of perceived improvement in various aspects of the college

information on the triggers. Also included in Table 1.2 is a column providing the results of statistical tests for differences in satisfaction levels between groups after the sample was split.

A multiple regression equation was designed to provide evidence of the predictive ability of the mediators on a global measure of job satisfaction among college faculty. The results indicated that the model was highly significant ($p < .0001$) and explained close to half (49.4 percent) of the variance of job satisfaction. The most highly predictive mediators were the work itself, salary, relationships with administration, student quality and relationships, and institutional climate and culture. To examine the impact of the triggers, comparisons between various subsets of the sample were derived, tested through analysis of variance techniques, and graphed. The results of the tests of significance (F-test) are included in Table 1.2. In addition, the effect of each of the triggers is displayed using boxplots, or box-and-whisker diagrams (see Figures 1.2 to 1.6) that provide a visual indication of the median response (vertical line) as well as the interquartile (25th to 75th percentile) range (width and location of box).

**Table 1.2. Tests of the Effects of Triggers
(Items from the NSOPF 1993)**

Trigger	How Defined	F-Test
Change in life stage	Sample split into 3 age groups: *Young*—35 and younger (15th percentile) *Middle Aged*—36 to 54 (16th to 75th percentile) *Senior*—55 and over (76th percentile)	9.973[*]
Change in family-related or personal circumstances	Sample split by marital status: *Single, never married* *Married* *Separated or divorced*	27.073[*]
Change in rank or tenure	Sample split between: *Recently promoted* *In rank for more than 5 years*	220.776[*]
Transfer to new institution	Sample split between: *At institution less than 4 years* *At institution 10 years or longer*	234.790[*]
Change in perceived justice	Sample split by responses regarding observa- tions of gender and ethnic prejudice: *Low* *High*	702.506
Change in mood or emotional state	Items measuring change in mood or emotional state not available	

Note: The dependent variable is Faculty Job Satisfaction, based on a scale measuring satisfaction with multiple aspects of the job at the institution.

[*]$p < .001$

Although there are differences in the distributions for job satisfaction among faculty as divided by the triggers, the boxplots demonstrate that the effects are subtle but certainly evident. It appears that on average, job satisfaction increases with advanced life stages (Figure 1.2) and can be affected by family-related circumstances with married faculty reporting higher levels of job satisfaction than either their single or divorced counterparts (Figure 1.3). Also, those who recently changed rank (Figure 1.4) or moved to a new institution (Figure 1.5) reported lower levels of job satisfaction, thus supplying some evidence that change may affect job satisfaction negatively. Finally, those faculty who perceived a high level of justice within their institutions reported much higher levels of job satisfaction than those whose perceptions of justice were low (Figure 1.6). Please note that although the scale of measurement for global job satisfaction in Figures 1.2 to 1.6 does not perfectly conform to the continuum of Figure 1.1 (disengagement, acceptance/tolerance, appreciation), a relationship is implied. The purpose

Figure 1.2. Global Job Satisfaction by Life Stages

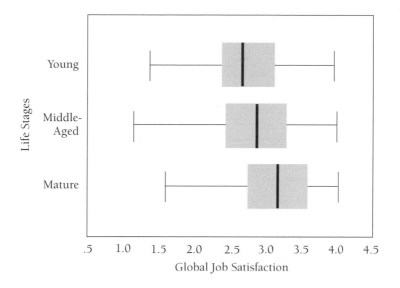

Figure 1.3. Global Job Satisfaction by Family-Related Circumstances

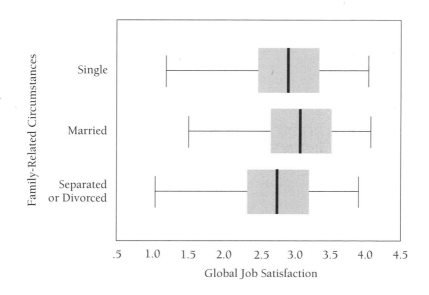

Figure 1.4. Global Job Satisfaction by Recent Change in Rank

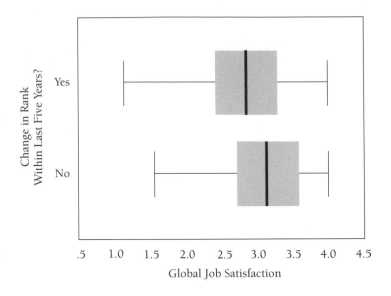

Figure 1.5. Global Job Satisfaction by Change in Institution

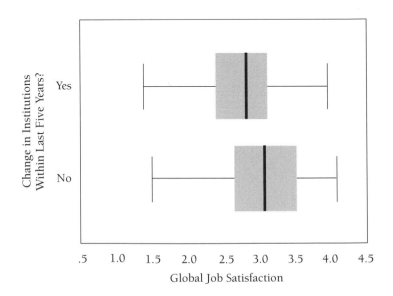

Figure 1.6. Global Job Satisfaction by Perceived Level of Justice

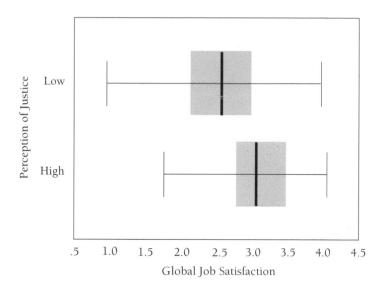

of the boxplots was not to make specific conclusions but rather to lend some credence to the hypothesized model. The statistical tests and graphs presented herein are not a substitute for extensive testing.

Conclusion

The present chapter opens this volume by introducing a general framework or model designed to help explain a substantial amount of the variance in faculty job satisfaction. While the statistical tests and graphs cannot prove that the framework is valid, they do lend support to the literature-based hypotheses from which the framework was derived. Although each individual has unique circumstances that must be encountered and incorporated in all facets of life, including the job, faculty share a commonality of purpose and profession that can be studied and better understood. The conceptual framework presented in this chapter is an aid to better understand the commonality that faculty share and provide a structure on which institutional analysis of job satisfaction can be based. Subsequent chapters of this volume look at job satisfaction and its outcomes through other lenses and for particular groups of faculty or staff.

References

Adams, G. A., King, L. A., and King, D. W. "Relationships of Job and Family Involvement, Family Social Support, and Work-Family Conflict with Job and Satisfaction." *Journal of Applied Psychology*, 1996, *81*, 411–420.

Baldwin, R. G. "Adult and Career Development: What Are the Implications for Faculty?" *Current Issues in Higher Education*, no. 2. Washington, D.C.: American Association for Higher Education, 1979.

Baldwin, R. G. "Faculty Career Stages and Implications for Professional Development." In J. H. Schuster, D. W. Wheeler, and Associates, *Enhancing Faculty Careers: Strategies for Development and Renewal.* San Francisco: Jossey-Bass, 1990.

Biglan, A. "The Characteristics of Subject Matter in Different Academic Areas." *Journal of Applied Psychology*, 1973a, *57*(3), 195–203.

Biglan, A. "Relationships Between Subject Matter Characteristics and the Structure and Output of University Departments." *Journal of Applied Psychology*, 1973b, *57*(3), 204–213.

Bloom, A. *The Closing of the American Mind.* New York: Simon & Schuster, 1987.

Braskamp, L. A., and Ory, J. C. "Faculty Development and Achievement: A Faculty's View." *Review of Higher Education*, 1984, *7*(3), 205–222.

Bullers, S. "Selection Effects in the Relationship Between Women's Work/Family Status and Perceived Control." *Family Relations: Interdisciplinary Journal of Applied Family Studies*, 1999, *48*(2), 181–188.

Carnevale, D. G., and Rios, J. M. "How Employees Assess the Quality of Physical Work Settings." *Public Productivity and Management Review*, 1995, *18*, 221–231.

Diener, T. "Job Satisfaction and College Faculty in Two Predominantly Black Institutions." *Journal of Negro Education*, 1985, *54*(4), 558–565.

Duxbury, L., Higgins, C., and Lee, C. "Impact of Life-Cycle Stage and Gender on the Ability to Balance Work and Family Responsibilities." *Family Relations*, 1994, *43*, 144–150.

Erikson, E. H. *Identity and the Life Cycle.* New York: Norton, 1979.

Erikson, E. H. *The Life Cycle Completed.* New York: Norton, 1997.

Furnham, A., Forde, L., and Ferrari, K. "Personality and Work Motivation." *Personality and Individual Differences*, 1999, *26*(6), 1035–1043.

Gallagher, W. E., Jr., and Einhorn, H. J. "Motivation Theory and Job Design." *Journal of Business*, 1976, *49*(3), 358–373.

Gawel, J. E. *Herzberg's Theory of Motivation and Maslow's Hierarchy of Needs.* Washington, D.C.: ERIC Clearinghouse on Assessment and Evaluation, 1997. (ED 421 486)

Hagedorn, L. S. "Retirement Proximity's Role in the Prediction of Satisfaction in Academe." *Research in Higher Education*, 1994, *35*(6), 711–728.

Hagedorn, L. S. "Wage Equity and Female Faculty Job Satisfaction: The Role of Wage Differentials in a Job Satisfaction Causal Model." *Research in Higher Education*, 1996, *37*(5), 569–598.

Hagedorn, L. S. "Implications to Postsecondary Faculty of Alternative Calculation Methods of Gender-Based Wage Differentials." *Research in Higher Education*, 1998, *39*(2), 143–162.

Hagedorn, L. S., and Sax, L. J. "The Role of Family Related Factors in Faculty Job Satisfaction." Paper presented at the annual meeting of the American Educational Research Association, 1999.

Harrigan, M. N. "An Analysis of Faculty Turnover at the University of Wisconsin–Madison." Paper presented at the Association for Institutional Research conference, Seattle, 1999.

Hemmasi, M., Graf, L. A., and Lust, J. A. "Correlates of Pay and Benefit Satisfaction: The Unique Case of Public University Faculty." *Public Personnel Management*, 1992, *21*(4), 442–443.

Hensel, N. *Realizing Gender Equality in Higher Education: The Need to Integrate Work/Family Issues.* ASHE-ERIC Higher Education Report no. 2. Washington, D.C.: School of Education and Human Development, George Washington University, 1991.

Herzberg, F., Mausner, B., Peterson, R. O., and Capwell, D. F. *Job Attitudes: Review of Research and Opinion.* Pittsburgh, Pa.: Psychological Services of Pittsburgh, 1957.

Herzberg, F., Mausner, B., and Snyderman, B. *The Motivation to Work.* (2nd rev. ed.) New York: Wiley, 1959.

Holder, J. C., and Vaux, A. "African American Professionals: Coping with Occupational Stress in Predominantly White Work Environments." *Journal of Vocational Behavior,* 1998, *53*(3), 315–333.

Holland, J. R. "A Nation at Risk." *Review of Higher Education,* 1985, *9*(1), 51–65.

Hutchins, R. M. *The Higher Learning in America.* New Haven, Conn.: Yale University Press, 1936.

Izard, C., Kagan, J., and Zajonc, R. *Emotions, Cognition, and Behavior.* New York: Cambridge University Press, 1984.

Jena, S.P.K. "Job, Life Satisfaction and Occupational Stress of Women." *Social Science International,* 1999, *15*(1), 75–80.

Kelly, J. D. "Gender, Pay and Job Satisfaction of Faculty in Journalism." *Journalism Quarterly,* 1989, *66*(2), 446–452.

Kimball, R. *Tenured Radicals: How Politics Has Corrupted Higher Education.* New York: HarperCollins, 1990.

Kirby, D., and Jackson, J. S. "Mitigating Perceptions of Racism: The Importance of Work Group Composition and Supervisor's Race." In A. J. Murrell and F. J. Crosby (eds.), *Mentoring Dilemmas: Developmental Relationships Within Multicultural Organizations.* Mahwah, N.J.: Erlbaum, 1999.

Knight, P. J., and Westbrook, J. "Comparing Employees in Traditional Job Structures Vs. Telecommuting Jobs Using Herzberg's Hygienes and Motivators." *Engineering Management Journal,* Mar. 1999, pp. 15–20.

Latack, J. C. "Career Transitions Within Organizations: An Exploratory Study of Work, Nonwork, and Coping Strategies." *Organizational Behavior and Human Decision Processes,* 1984, *34*(3), 296–322.

Levinson, D. J. *Seasons of a Man's Life.* New York: Knopf, 1978.

Levinson, D. J. *Seasons of a Woman's Life.* New York: Knopf, 1996.

National Center for Education Statistics. *1993 National Study of Postsecondary Faculty.* Sponsored by the Office of Educational Research and Improvement, U.S. Department of Education. Co-sponsored by the National Science Foundation and National Endowment for the Humanities. Washington, D.C.: National Center for Education Statistics, 1993.

Neugarten, B. L. *The Meanings of Age.* Chicago: University of Chicago Press, 1996.

Niemann, Y. F., and Dovidio, J. F. "Relationship of Solo Status, Academic Rank, and Perceived Distinctiveness to Job Satisfaction of Racial/Ethnic Minorities." *Journal of Applied Psychology,* 1998, *83*(1), 55–71.

Olsen, D., Maple, S. A., and Stage, F. K. "Women and Minority Faculty Job Satisfaction: Professional Role, Interests, Professional Satisfactions, and Institutional Fit." *Journal of Higher Education,* 1995, *66*(3), 267–293.

Sheehy, G. *Passages.* New York: Bantam, 1976.

Sheehy, G. *New Passages.* New York: Random House, 1995.

Smart, J. C. "A Causal Model of Faculty Turnover Intentions." *Research in Higher Education,* 1990, *31*(5), 405–424.

Sowell, T. *Inside American Education: The Decline, the Deception, the Dogmas.* New York: Free Press, 1993.

Stark, J. S. "Classifying Professional Preparation Programs." *Journal of Higher Education,* 1998, *69*(4), 353–383.

Sykes, C. J. *ProfScam: Professors and the Demise of Higher Education.* Washington, D.C.: Regnery, 1988.

Tack, M. W., and Patitu, C. L. *Faculty Job Satisfaction: Women and Minorities in Peril.* Washington, D.C.: School of Education and Human Development, George Washington University, 1992.

Waskel, S. A., and Owens, R. "Frequency Distribution of Trigger Events Identified by People Ages 30 Through 60." *College Student Journal,* 1991, 25(2), 235–239.

Weiss, H. M., Nicholas, J. P., and Daus, C. S. "An Examination of the Joint Effects of Affective Experiences and Job Beliefs on Job Satisfaction and Variations in Affective Experiences over Time." *Organizational Behavior and Human Decision Processes,* 1999, 78(1), 1–24.

Wren, D. A., and Greenwood, R. G. *Management Innovators: The People and Ideas That Shaped Modern Business.* New York: Oxford University Press, 1998.

Young, C. "Emotions and Emotional Intelligence." [http://trochim.human.cornell.edu /gallery/young/emotion.htm]. 1996.

LINDA SERRA HAGEDORN is associate professor of higher education and senior research associate at the Center for Higher Education Policy Analysis at the University of Southern California. She is also chair of the Community College Leadership program.

2

Using autobiographical accounts written by women educators to consider the ways in which they derive satisfaction, the author suggests useful approaches for assessing campus climates in order to facilitate the satisfaction of women faculty members.

Aren't You Satisfied Yet? Women Faculty Members' Interpretations of Their Academic Work

Becky Ropers-Huilman

> Women are, historically, quite recent immigrants to the academic groves; we are still anomalies . . . in the sense that western academic tradition is grounded in male notions of reality and knowledge, including the notion that all that is female must be excised from the world of intellect. Yet a woman teaching is surely in her oldest element, doing classic women's work—raising the young. We are thus in a wonderfully ambiguous position, in place and out of place, marginal and central.
> —Gail B. Griffin (1992, p. ix)

Literature focusing on gendered experiences suggests that women's lives have often been either excluded from analyses of social conditions, or misinterpreted when a typically male pattern of life is used as the norm (Gilligan, 1982; Spender, 1992). From a historical view, literature also demonstrates that many higher education environments have not fully embraced women teachers, learners, and leaders (Aisenberg and Harrington, 1988; Chamberlain, 1988; Horowitz, 1987; Park, 1996; Rich, 1993). In particular, women with progressive or feminist commitments, because they often work against the norms of university life in some ways, struggle to gain full acceptance in the academic groves (Griffin, 1992; Hollingsworth, Schmuck, and Lock, 1998; Kolodny, 1998; Lewis, 1993; Middleton, 1993; Ropers-Huilman, 1998). Due to the ambiguous position resulting from these conditions, factors mitigating faculty satisfaction might be different for women—especially

21

those who assert the importance of social justice or feminism in their work. In this chapter, I review the ways in which academic women, writing auto-biographically about their lives, articulated the conditions of their satisfaction with their work lives.

Scholars have suggested several indicators for faculty satisfaction. In one review of literature, Linda Serra Hagedorn (1996) determined that these can be categorized as: (1) salary levels, (2) tenure and rank, (3) perceived support and interactions with superiors or facilitators, (4) job stress, (5) interaction with students, (6) social aspects and collegial relations, and (7) the "person-environment" fit, or satisfaction with the institution (pp. 571–572). Although useful, it is possible that a gendered analysis might allow other indicators to emerge that have heretofore not been identified or understood in terms of their roles in women faculty members' lives.

For example, through a review of relevant literature and interviews with female faculty, Riger, Stokes, Raja, and Sullivan (1997) identified six factors that they suspected would affect the satisfaction of women in academic working environments: (1) dual standards and opportunities, (2) sexist attitudes and comments, (3) informal socializing, (4) balancing work and personal obligations, (5) remediation policies and practices, and (6) mentoring (pp. 66–67). Further, Annette Kolodny (1998) wrote that while she is unaware of a wide-scale effort to understand female faculty members' satisfaction, the anecdotal evidence she has heard suggests that some women faculty struggle with colleagues who are not familiar with their research, hidden workload issues, the lack of access to informal male networks, differential standards applied to evaluate their work, and inappropriate statements by external referees in the evaluation of their tenure packages. Still, Kolodny points out, literature focusing on the faculty satisfaction of women is currently scant and, often, speculative.

Methods of Analysis

This paper considers several published works, most autobiographical, that focus on how women faculty members construct and experience their academic lives. More specifically, I use autobiographical accounts written by women educators in higher education institutions to consider the ways in which they derive satisfaction. I conclude with suggestions for institutional researchers about useful approaches for assessing campus climates to facilitate the satisfaction of women faculty members.

Although much has been written on women's roles in higher education (for example, Aisenberg and Harrington, 1988; Chamberlain, 1988; Chlinwiak, 1997; Glazer-Raymo, 1999; Hensel, 1991; Lewis, 1993; Moore and Sagaria, 1991; Welch, 1990), several recent texts focus on women's own interpretations of their roles as faculty members, leaders, and change agents in higher education (de Castell and Bryson, 1997; Kolodny, 1998; Neumann and Peterson, 1997; Richardson, 1997). For this chapter, I analyzed three autobiographical texts: Laurel Richardson's *Fields of Play: Constructing an Academic Life* (1997); Gail Griffin's *Calling: Essays on Teaching in the Mother Tongue* (1992); and Anna Neumann and Penelope Peterson's edited anthology *Learning from Our Lives: Women, Research, and Autobiography in Education* (1997), containing autobiographical accounts from eleven prominent faculty members in the field of education. Additionally, I include data from two qualitative studies that involved women faculty members: William G. Tierney and Estela M. Bensimon's *Promotion and Tenure: Community and Socialization in Academe* (1996) and my book entitled *Feminist Teaching in Theory and Practice: Situating Power and Knowledge in Poststructural Classrooms* (Ropers-Huilman, 1998).

Women Faculty Members' Satisfaction

While grouping the findings of this analysis in categories derived from the texts, I did not attempt to match my analysis with preexisting categories suggested by the literature. Instead, I allowed for new indicators—or new definitions or interpretations of preexisting indicators. The indicators that I found which related to women faculty members' satisfaction were: ability to engage in scholarship for social change, teaching and learning relationships, colleagues and collaboration, and coherency. In this paper, I touch briefly on each of these potential indicators of faculty satisfaction, and then focus attention on the institutional research practices that are suggested by this analysis.

Ability to Engage in Scholarship for Social Change. Women faculty members derived satisfaction not only from their research but also from the knowledge of having their scholarship improve society. This is not a new finding, since others have determined that women faculty members tend to engage in scholarly activities that are action-oriented (Astin and Davis, 1993) and that feminist faculty members often express "the desire to integrate such feminist values as nurturance, mutuality, cooperation, and reciprocity into their scholarship and to select topics and methods that reflect their commitments to other women, their communities and to equality and social justice" (Dickens and Sagaria, 1997, p. 93). Many women wrote of the pull to conduct meaningful research that reflected their commitments to working for positive social change. For example, Concha Delgado-Gaitan (1997) wrote, "My research is as much a statement of my action in the world as was my teaching and leadership work" (p. 45).

Many women faculty members wrote that they derived great satisfaction from their scholarship. Their own measure of success for their scholarship, they asserted, was based on more than number of publications or acceptance of brilliance by colleagues. Instead, they were interested in how their scholarship could work toward positive social change, often serving various communities of people. They acknowledged that the academy was not always the easiest place in which to conduct this work, yet they asserted that the function or purpose of their scholarship was of utmost importance.

Teaching and Learning Relationships. Teaching and learning relationships that the women faculty members formed with their students were important to their satisfaction. For example, one feminist teacher discussed how she relied on relationships that formed in a graduate class: "I really look forward to a time in the week . . . when I know that intellectually I'll be stimulated and I'm going to receive something in return. . . . In many ways my solace, if you will, intellectually is not only the time I have by myself but [also the time in class]—this class has become a wonderful place for me. And I realized that yesterday, I was thinking, oh good—I get to go to class" (Ropers-Huilman, 1998, p. 69).

On the other side, though, several expressed frustrations related to their teaching and learning relationships and pointed out that the academic environment poses unique challenges for women faculty members in relation to their teaching roles. For example, women struggle with pressure to be academic mommies, taking care of graduate students and other departmental housekeeping functions (Griffin, 1992; Jipson, 1995; Park, 1996; Thorne and Hochschild, 1997). They often receive evaluations of their teaching that encompass a wide range of physical attributes and clothing styles, in addition to questions of competence (Griffin, 1992; Ng, 1997). They experience differential treatment from their students, being called by their first names while male faculty are addressed as "Doctor" and struggling with the familiarity, hierarchy, and sexism that this implies (Collison, 1999; Griffin, 1992).

Women faculty members seemed to take their relationships with students very seriously. While some women related purely to the enjoyment or frustration of their work with students, others referred to satisfaction as it related to the ability to make a difference in students' lives. For example, Gail Griffin (1992) wrote that, in teaching: "You become highly attuned to the power of voices. A woman student comes to see you, distraught. Dr. X has said her idea for a Senior Project is 'not really very serious.' . . . When she leaves, smiling, full of thanks, you know that you have exerted considerable power. You are amazed that you can do it. You are disturbed that you have had to do it" (p. 172). For Griffin, a key part of her teaching became "passing on tools for survival" (p. 73).

In sum, women faculty members found both great pleasure and frustration in their teaching and learning relationships. Many asserted that they viewed their teaching roles not merely as disseminating disciplinary information. Instead, they saw teaching as an opportunity—and obligation—to work toward social change with their students.

Colleagues and Collaborators. Previous research has consistently suggested that the quality of collegial relationships is a substantial indicator of satisfaction for faculty members (Hagedorn, 1996; Riger, Stokes, Raja, and Sullivan, 1997). Women faculty members tend to view connections with others who share similar interests or experiences as important for their success and happiness in their academic positions (Astin and Davis, 1993). These connections have shown to be important not only for satisfaction, but also for academic success in that women's groups often provide mentoring to beginning academics (Tierney and Bensimon, 1996), support each other's scholarship (Dickens and Sagaria, 1997), and provide a network of allies (Richardson, 1997). Connections or collaborations can take a variety of forms, many of which are directly instrumental to research, teaching, and service. In this review, I found additional evidence to support the importance of relationships with colleagues and collaborators.

Beyond academic functions, though, the reflections of these women faculty also suggest that the academic community forged through these connections with others leads to greater satisfaction. While considering the additional commitments that these connections often entail, Laurel Richardson (1997) wrote: "Academic community entails commitment to others, involvement with others' projects and products, a willingness to suspend one's individual needs, for a while, for the betterment of the whole. To tithe time, as it were. Without each of us giving, gracefully, to each other, how could either the community or our individual contributions be sustained? How awful I would feel if I were totally disconnected from this community: if no one asked me to do anything anymore" (p. 85).

Importantly, having colleagues' respect for their professional choices about which academic roles to play was crucial to women faculty members' satisfaction. Some women expressed dissatisfaction with colleagues attempting to determine the ways in which they performed their academic roles. One faculty member explained: "[I was] getting slammed [by colleagues] for being ideological and political in the classroom. They said my teaching could be supplemented by more authority-centered criticism, meaning that instead of allowing student voices, I should lecture. It rankled me. I was angry. I thought they would respect my work" (Tierney and Bensimon, 1996, p. 90). Women faculty members' satisfaction relied, in part, on their ability to perform the roles that they wanted to play in academe, and their colleagues' support of research, teaching, and service efforts that may not be traditional.

Dickens and Sagaria (1997) assert that women's exclusion from networks is detrimental to their professional advancement, yet increasing women's participation in networks mandates a revision of those networks such that women faculty members are allowed and encouraged to determine their own professional roles. Some of the women faculty members in this review seemed up to the challenge of working to change academic environments and the networks that differentially support their participants. In Linda Winfield's (1997) words, "I realize the value of informing, not only the research process and knowledge production but also the process of higher education more broadly, from my unique perspective as an African American female" (p. 207). If faculty members choose to play that role, and if that role is valued, it may increase women faculty members' satisfaction.

A Coherent Life. Coherency between the various aspects of life, as broadly construed, was noted or demonstrated by nearly all of the women faculty members whose work I reviewed. For example, many women faculty members spoke of the ways they envisioned their family and work experiences as complementing each other. These reflections often went beyond the category of "balancing work and family responsibilities" that is found in the literature (Riger, Stokes, Raja, and Sullivan, 1997). Instead, several faculty members reflected on the ways that their involvement in and support from a family strengthened their academic work. Gloria Ladson-Billings (1997) describes how the scientific notion of objectivity doesn't make sense because of the coherency in her life. "I deliberately write this narrative within and outside of my personal life because I believe that my personal life (or who I am as a person) informs and shapes who I am as a scholar. I resist notions of myself as an 'objective' researcher when what I research is so intricately linked to the life I have lived and continue to live" (p. 52). In many of these narratives, women faculty members asserted that the connections they formed with—and the lessons they learned from—their families and communities supported the academic work that they were able to do.

Even though women faculty members believed that their dual roles as family and faculty members strengthened their academic work, some were given the message that their desire to have children was not welcomed by their departmental colleagues. One woman described that while her department seemed to be accepting of one child, she received a clear message that her second child was seen as a mistake (Tierney and Bensimon, 1996, p. 91). These types of experiences, combined with the perception that child rearing might be a career impediment, may be why 61 percent of assistant professors in one study identified "time for children" as an impediment to achieving tenure (Finkel and Olswang, 1996).

The women faculty members whose reflections I reviewed for this paper also expressed a desire to have coherency between their work and the communities in which they were situated. As one faculty member told me, "My goal is that my teaching, my research, and my service all serve people who are not served well in this country" (Ropers-Huilman, 1998, p. 150). Like the coherency between work and family, the women faculty who discussed this type of coherency also asserted that it strengthened their academic work. To the extent that they were seen as persons with complementary lives outside the academy, women faculty members' satisfaction was strengthened. Patricia Gumport's (1997) words reflect a sentiment that seemed to permeate many of the beliefs of women faculty members: "To the extent that I choose between making sense and seeking approval, I choose making sense. . . . In a world where approval and what we most care about are not at odds, the form of our lives and our work will be richer reflections of ourselves" (pp. 191–192).

Discussion

The women faculty members who wrote the texts that I reviewed did not interpret their academic lives in identical ways. They pointed out that their backgrounds, ethnicities, epistemologies, areas of scholarship, family situations, disciplinary affiliations, departments, colleagues, and students (to name but a few) all had differential effects on the ways that they experienced their work. However, many of their autobiographical accounts stressed that their satisfaction related to their ability to engage in scholarship for social change, teaching and learning relationships, collegial and collaborative relationships, and their ability to develop personal and professional lives that felt coherent.

Based on this review, institutional researchers and other educational leaders may want to consider the following in their analyses of campus climates for women faculty members.

Recognize the benefits of "starting thought from women's lives." Sandra Harding (1993) writes of the benefits of starting thought from women's lives because they are often marginalized in social settings in which they are involved. This outside-looking-in position allows them to see structures that might be so ingrained that those who are well entrenched in the system might not see. In other words, it is hard to see, describe, and dismantle a barrier that one has never bumped into. Maxine Greene (1997), recent recipient of a lifetime achievement award in education, wrote of feeling marginal to the various disciplines in which she contributed. Laurel Richardson (1997), full professor of sociology at Ohio State University, wrote of experiencing her life as "far from normal," but still being "comfortable on the (intellectual, sociological) margins" (p. 150). Laurie Fink (quoted in Maher and Tetreault, 1994) pointed out that "What is perceived as marginal at any given time depends on the position one occupies" (p. 164). Institutional research would benefit from the perspectives of those who have a variety of background experiences and institutional perspectives. Women's interpretations of their own experiences may prove a valuable resource for an institution that is serious about assessing and improving the campus climate for women faculty.

Seek out the assistance of women's and feminist groups in conducting research, and reward their participation. Seeking out assistance from individual women and from women's and feminist groups may prove useful in assessing the campus climate for women and in attempting to change that climate. Commissions may also facilitate positive change on college campuses (Glazer-Raymo, 1999). As is evidenced from this analysis, at least some women are attempting to understand how their lives as women can coexist with their lives as faculty members. They are "inside" the question, so to speak. Seeking help from women who are also feminists may provide an additional benefit. Feminists on campus might be able to aid an institutional assessment and provide recommendations that are both well grounded in literature and specific to an individual campus climate. Their outsider-within (Collins, 1991) position may help with a thorough analysis. It is important that women's and feminist groups on a particular campus be involved in these efforts, and that they be rewarded for this important service to the institution.

Recognize women's multiple identity characteristics and value their result-ing contributions. It is important to recognize that all women have multiple identity characteristics that shape how they view their academic work. Women faculty members in the texts that I reviewed for this work often attempted to create coherency between those parts of their lives. Research should refrain from perceiving women as representative of only one part of their identities, and rather should consider how those parts interact to func-tion as a dynamic whole. In developing their recommendations, those doing institutional research may find it useful to heed Eric Dey's (1994) advice relating to reducing stress in the academy. He writes, "Rather than taking a 'one size fits all' approach, institutions should pay attention to the stressors that affect different groups of faculty" (p. 320). Researchers should further recognize that for some female scholars, particularly those who are also per-sons of color, lesbians, or from a working-class background, the question of satisfaction seems to be putting the cart in front of the horse. Although sat-isfaction, stress, and survival are interrelated, stress and survival must be attended to when considering satisfaction.

Research could also help others understand and possibly advocate for the value of social justice work that encompasses or relates to these multi-ple positions. Some women are strongly committed to women's studies or minority studies, or to students, colleagues, or community groups with sim-ilar demographic characteristics. Rather than perceiving that these com-mitments might be decreasing these women's ability to make valued scholarly contributions (Astin and Davis, 1993; Park, 1996), institutional research could facilitate a broad examination of the varied types of contri-butions that women faculty members make to their campus, disciplinary, and other social communities.

Attend to both institutional structures and individual interactions. Both individual interactions and institutional structures shape the campus envi-ronment in which women are expected to compose their academic lives. If a policy on sexual harassment clearly dictates the bounds of appropriate relationships between male and female employees but is enforced only grudgingly, women's satisfaction and job performance may be negatively affected. As Laurel Richardson (1997) articulated, "People make sense of their lives, for the most part, in terms of specific events . . . and sequences of events. . . . Most people do not articulate how sociological categories such as race, gender, class, and ethnicity have shaped their lives" (p. 15). Research on the campus climate should attend to the ways in which both broad-scale and local factors shape the satisfaction that women experience, and consider how those factors magnify or diminish the effects of others.

Attend to general themes—such as scholarship, teaching and learning, colle-gial relationships, and coherency—while also considering campus-specific inter-pretations of those experiences. The women faculty members whose reflections were reviewed for this work, while having unique experiences, were largely similar in several ways. First, most were well established by many academic definitions—many were tenured professors at prominent research universities in the United States. Second, most were in the social sciences or in education. It is useful to review literature that could provide suggestions for assessing the campus climate for women faculty members. However, such a broad analysis should not replace a localized assessment of a particular campus.

Gather quantitative and qualitative data from various sources. Some important questions to ask include the following:

- How many women and men hold key administrative (including vice president, dean, and chairperson) or committee appointments?
- How many women and men hold tenured faculty lines?
- What is the pattern of success in tenure and promotion among men and women?
- Who has received public recognition and reward for their contributions to the institution in the past five years? What prompted that recognition?
- What are the salary differentials between men and women at similar levels?
- Are the service and teaching responsibilities allocated equally among women and men?
- How many women have been assaulted or harassed in the institution?
- How many women have used resources designed to meet women's or families' needs (women's center, women's groups, campus child care facilities, and so on) or would have used them had they existed?
- How do women who view their work as part of their commitment to social justice fare in the above questions?
- How do women who are also part of a racial or sexual minority group, or who have a disability, fare in the above questions?

In many ways, it would be useful for institutional researchers to go beyond single-source data collection techniques in their assessments. Would the information about assaults on women provided by women's center or health center employees on campus be the same as that provided by the police? Even gathering quantitative data from multiple sources, though, should be balanced with qualitative inquiry to better understand the complexities of women faculty members' satisfaction. Quantitative data may suggest unique problems and strengths of a particular campus that need additional qualitative research for a more thorough understanding.

Be prepared to solicit feedback, listen, and make recommendations that may alter the academic structure in significant ways. Clearly, efforts to enhance campus climates for women are not new. From curriculum transformation (Andersen, 1988; Friedman, Kolmar, Flint, and Rothenberg, 1996; Minnich, 1990) to assessing and redressing the "chilly climate" (Hall and Sandler, 1982; Sadker and Sadker, 1994) to taking up sexual harassment as a serious offense (Hagedorn, 1999; Sandler and Shoop, 1997), efforts have been made to alter sexist conditions. There are opportunities for positive change and growth in the academy. Literature proposes some ways to facilitate that growth. For example, Susan Twombly (1999) asserts, "We now know that both training and restructuring are necessary but insufficient for organizations to shed their patriarchal ways and to become more 'peoplearchal'" (p. 446). In working to change systems and environments that have negative effects on women and others who are underrepresented in the academy, institutional researchers may be in a unique position to identify and influence policies and practices that might have differential effects for faculty members based, in part, on gender. Based on quantitative and qualitative data, policies and practices could be reformed to foster and acknowledge the contributions of women faculty members and, consequently, increase their satisfaction.

We must address the sources of satisfaction for women and feminist faculty. In this way, we will ensure that groups who are interested in facilitating positive social change through relationships on college campuses feel welcome enough to stay and do the work.

References

Aisenberg, N., and Harrington, M. *Women of Academe: Outsiders in the Sacred Grove.* Amherst: University of Massachusetts, 1988.

Andersen, M. L. "Changing the Curriculum in Higher Education." In E. Minnich, J. O'Barr, and R. Rosenfeld (eds.), *Reconstructing the Academy: Women's Education and Women's Studies.* Chicago: University of Chicago, 1988.

Astin, H. S., and Davis, D. E. "Research Productivity Across the Life and Career Cycles: Facilitators and Barriers for Women." In J. S. Glazer, E. M. Bensimon, and B. K. Townsend (eds.), *Women in Higher Education: A Feminist Perspective.* Needham Heights, Mass.: Ginn, 1993.

Chamberlain, M. K. *Women in Academe: Progress and Prospects.* New York: Russell Sage Foundation, 1988.

Chlinwiak, L. *Higher Education Leadership: Analyzing the Gender Gap.* ASHE-ERIC Higher Education Report, vol. 25, no. 4. Washington, D.C.: Graduate School of Education and Human Development, George Washington University, 1997.

Collins, P. H. *Black Feminist Thought: Knowledge, Consciousness, and the Politics of Empowerment.* New York: Routledge, 1991.

Collison, M. N.-K. "Earning and Demanding." *Black Issues in Higher Education,* May 29, 1999, pp. 30–31.

de Castell, S., and Bryson, M. *Radical Interventions: Identity, Politics and Differences in Educational Praxis.* Albany: State University of New York, 1997.

Delgado-Gaitan, C. "Dismantling Borders." In A. Neumann and P. Peterson (eds.), *Learning from Our Lives: Women, Research, and Autobiography in Education.* New York: Teachers College Press, 1997.

Dey, E. "Dimensions of Faculty Stress: A Recent Survey." *Review of Higher Education,* 1994, *17*(3), 305–322.

Dickens, C. S., and Sagaria, M.A.D. "Feminists at Work: Collaborative Relationships Among Women Faculty." *Review of Higher Education,* 1997, *21*(1), 79–101.

Finkel, S. K., and Olswang, S. G. "Child Rearing as a Career Impediment to Women Assistant Professors." *Review of Higher Education,* 1996, *19*(2), 123–139.

Friedman, E. G., Kolmar, W. K., Flint, C. B., and Rothenberg, P. *Creating an Inclusive College Curriculum.* New York: Teachers College Press, 1996.

Gilligan, C. *In a Different Voice: Psychological Theory and Women*. Boston: Harvard University Press, 1982.

Glazer-Raymo, J. *Shattering the Myths: Women in Academe*. Baltimore: Johns Hopkins University Press, 1999.

Greene, M. "Exclusions and Awakenings." In A. Neumann and P. Peterson (eds.), *Learning from Our Lives: Women, Research, and Autobiography in Education*. New York: Teachers College Press, 1997.

Griffin, G. B. *Calling: Essays on Teaching in the Mother Tongue*. Pasadena, Calif.: Trilogy Books, 1992.

Gumport, P. "First Words. Still Words." In A. Neumann and P. Peterson (eds.), *Learning from Our Lives: Women, Research, and Autobiography in Education*. New York: Teachers College Press, 1997.

Hagedorn, L. S. "Wage Equity and Female Faculty Job Satisfaction: The Role of Wage Differentials in a Job Satisfaction Causal Model." *Research in Higher Education*, 1996, 37(5), 569–598.

Hagedorn, L. S. "Cruel Environments: Sexual Abuse and Harassment in the Academy." *Higher Education: Handbook of Theory and Research*, 1999, 14, 398–436.

Hall, R. M., and Sandler, B. R. *The Classroom Climate: A Chilly One for Women*. Washington, D.C.: Project on the Status and Education of Women, Association of American Colleges, 1982.

Harding, S. "Starting Thought from Women's Lives: Eight Resources for Maximizing Objectivity." In J. S. Glazer, E. M. Bensimon, and B. K. Townsend (eds.), *Women in Higher Education: A Feminist Perspective*. Needham Heights, Mass.: Ginn, 1993.

Hensel, N. *Realizing Gender Equality in Higher Education: The Need to Integrate Work/Family Issues*. ASHE-ERIC Higher Education Report no. 2. Washington, D.C.: School of Education and Human Development, George Washington University, 1991.

Hollingsworth, S., Schmuck, P., and Lock, R. "Women Administrators and the Point of Exit: Collision Between the Person and the Institution." Paper presented at the American Educational Research Association conference, San Diego, Calif., 1998.

Horowitz, H. L. *Campus Life: Undergraduate Cultures from the End of the Eighteenth Century to the Present*. Chicago: University of Chicago Press, 1987.

Jipson, J. "Teacher-Mother: An Imposition of Identity." In J. Jipson, P. Munro, S. Victor, K. F. Jones, and G. Freed-Rowland (eds.), *Repositioning Feminism and Education: Perspectives on Educating for Social Change*. Westport, Conn.: Bergin & Garvey, 1995.

Kolodny, A. *Failing the Future: A Dean Looks at the Twenty-First Century*. Durham, N.C.: Duke, 1998.

Ladson-Billings, G. "For Colored Girls Who Have Considered Suicide When the Academy's Not Enough: Reflections of an African American Woman Scholar." In A. Neumann and P. Peterson (eds.), *Learning from Our Lives: Women, Research, and Autobiography in Education*. New York: Teachers College Press, 1997.

Lewis, M. G. *Without a Word: Teaching Beyond Women's Silence*. New York: Routledge, 1993.

Maher, F. A., and Tetreault, M.K.T. *The Feminist Classroom*. New York: Basic Books, 1994.

Middleton, S. *Educating Feminists: Life Histories and Pedagogy*. New York: Teachers College Press, 1993.

Minnich, E. K. *Transforming Knowledge*. Philadelphia: Temple University, 1990.

Moore, K. M., and Sagaria, M.A.D. "The Situation of Women in Research Universities in the United States: Within the Inner Circles of Academic Power." In G. P. Kelly and S. Slaughter (eds.), *Women's Higher Education in Comparative Perspective*. Norwell, Mass.: Kluwer, 1991.

Neumann, A., and Peterson, P. (eds.). *Learning from Our Lives: Women, Research, and Autobiography in Education*. New York: Teachers College Press, 1997.

Ng, R. "A Woman Out of Control: Deconstructing Sexism and Racism in the University." In S. de Castell and M. Bryson (eds.), *Radical Interventions: Identity, Politics and Differences in Educational Praxis*. Albany: State University of New York, 1997.

Park, S. M. "Research, Teaching, and Service: Why Shouldn't Women's Work Count?" *Journal of Higher Education,* 1996, 67(1), 46–84.

Rich, A. "Toward a Woman-Centered University." In J. S. Glazer, E. M. Bensimon, and B. K. Townsend (eds.), *Women in Higher Education: A Feminist Perspective.* Needham Heights, Mass.: Ginn, 1993.

Richardson, L. *Fields of Play: Constructing an Academic Life.* New York: Routledge, 1997.

Riger, S., Stokes, J., Raja, S., and Sullivan, M. "Measuring Perceptions of the Work Environment for Female Faculty." *Review of Higher Education,* 1997, 21(1), 63–78.

Ropers-Huilman, B. *Feminist Teaching in Theory and Practice: Situating Power and Knowledge in Poststructural Classrooms.* New York: Teachers College Press, 1998.

Sadker, M., and Sadker, D. *Failing at Fairness: How America's Schools Cheat Girls.* New York: Scribner, 1994.

Sandler, B. R., and Shoop, R. J. *Sexual Harassment on Campus: A Guide for Administrators, Faculty, and Students.* Needham Heights, Mass.: Allyn & Bacon, 1997.

Spender, D. "The Entry of Women to the Education of Men." In C. Kramarae and D. Spender (eds.), *The Knowledge Explosion: Generations of Feminist Scholarship.* New York: Teachers College Press, 1992.

Thorne, B., and Hochschild, A. R. "Feeling at Home at Work: Life in Academic Departments." *Qualitative Sociology,* 1997, 20(4), 517–520.

Tierney, W. G., and Bensimon, E. M. *Promotion and Tenure: Community and Socialization in Academe.* Albany: State University of New York, 1996.

Twombly, S. B. "New Scholarship on Academic Women: Beyond 'Women's Ways.'" *Review of Higher Education,* 1999, 22(4), 441–454.

Welch, L. B. *Women in Higher Education: Changes and Challenges.* New York: Praeger, 1990.

Winfield, L. F. "Multiple Dimensions of Reality: Recollections of an African American Woman Scholar." In A. Neumann and P. Peterson (eds.), *Learning from Our Lives: Women, Research, and Autobiography in Education.* New York: Teachers College Press, 1997.

BECKY ROPERS-HUILMAN is assistant professor of higher education and women's and gender studies at Louisiana State University in Baton Rouge.

3

This chapter describes the challenges of academic
medicine and proposes a model of faculty satisfaction.
In addition, the chapter discusses the elements of
satisfaction in academic medicine.

Faculty Satisfaction in Academic Medicine

Julie G. Nyquist, Maurice A. Hitchcock, Arianne Teherani

Faculty in academic medicine have been pivotal in the improvement of quality and length of life in this century through the discovery of new diagnostic techniques and therapeutics, the training of the next generation of doctors, and the care of patients (often the poor). Faculty of medical schools have contributed boldly to the advancement of medicine and the well-being of mankind. This chapter deals with a definition of these faculty, describes what they do, and finally addresses what affects their satisfaction.

Who are medical academics? In 1997 there were 257,522 faculty (95,440 full-time) within the 126 medical schools in the United States. Faculty in schools of medicine can be divided into two overall categories, basic science and clinical. Basic science faculty make up about 18 percent of the full-time faculty and 10 percent of the entire medical faculty (full-time, part-time, and voluntary) (Jolly and Hudley, 1998), are generally housed in universities, and teach medical students during their first two (preclinical) years of training. Their job roles and responsibilities are similar to those of other science faculty in research universities.

The clinical faculty is composed primarily of physicians holding the M.D. degree. These faculty make up the remaining 82 percent of the full-time faculty and 90 percent of the entire medical faculty (full-time, part-time, and voluntary) (Jolly and Hudley, 1998). Most clinical faculty work within academic medical centers (AMCs) that are affiliated with the Council of Teaching Hospitals and Health Systems. In 1995 there were 362 AMCs, 114 integrated with schools of medicine, 160 independent hospitals, 69 Veterans Administration Hospitals, and 19 Children's Hospitals (Jolly and Hudley, 1998). In this chapter, we focus primarily on the clinical faculty within AMCs.

33

Academic Medicine: Turmoil Within a Paradigm Shift

AMCs pursue three primary missions: (1) educating and training physicians, medical scientists, and other health professionals; (2) performing basic and clinical biomedical research, including the development of new technologies and procedures; and (3) delivering patient care, often for the poorest and most seriously ill patients (Kassirer, 1994; Heinig, Quon, Meyer, and Korn, 1999). Although the core missions of academic medicine have not changed over the past decade, all three are threatened by the changing business of medicine.

Beginning in the early 1990s articles and position papers began to appear which described the stresses within AMCs and the deleterious effects on faculty and their work (Burrow, 1993; Genel and others, 1996; Greisler, 1998; Kassirer, 1994; Korn, 1996; Swick, 1998). Genel and colleagues (1996) said "The need for 'reengineering' or 'downsizing' of academic medical centers has led to great faculty distress and trainee confusion." In a 1998 article in *Academic Medicine,* Mitchell Rabkin described twenty-five changes in academic medicine resulting in a true paradigm shift. Academic medicine remains in the midst of this change.

Growth of Academic Medicine. Prior to World War II, AMCs focused primarily on teaching and patient care. Research activities were small and funded either internally or by foundations and industry (Korn, 1996). In support of the war effort during World War II, the government began to provide funding for university laboratories, leading to a huge expansion of AMCs after the war (Korn, 1996; Greisler, 1998). Federal legislation during the 1960s resulted in enactment of the Medicare and Medicaid programs, which further fueled the expansions. Medicare also provided direct financial support for graduate medical education—the three to seven years of advanced training after medical school that results in specialists in all fields of medicine. Academic medicine thrived during these times of abundant resources. American AMCs became world-renowned tertiary care centers focusing on research, teaching, and the care of the most seriously ill patients (Burrow, 1993; Pardes, 1997).

Cross-Subsidization and Growth of the Clinical Educator. In 1976 clinical practice income accounted for just 12 percent of medical school revenue. Most faculty in medical schools fit the following profile: white, male, board-certified subspecialists devoting large amounts of time to scholarly pursuits and education. This clinician-scientist typically spent only 10 to 20 percent of time in direct patient care, usually with students present. Faculty in the surgical specialties divided this time between the operating room, ward, and clinic. Nonsurgical faculty often saw patients for one or two half-days per week in an outpatient clinic and supervised residents in an inpatient setting one to three months per year (Levinson and Rubinstein, 1999). The other 80 to 90 percent of the physician faculty member's time was typically spent in research (Rosenberg, 1999; Levinson and Rubinstein, 1999).

AMCs were growing and sought to increase their clinical revenue as tuition, research and training grants, and state and local governmental support remained fairly level. This could not be done without a change in the mix of faculty. Thus, clinician-educator tracks began to develop. The clinician-educator has historically been a full-time AMC clinical faculty member in a promotional track that does not grant tenure. These faculty spend approximately 50 percent of their time in direct patient care (often with students) and the rest of their time organizing and implementing educational activities (Levinson and Rubinstein, 1999). Surveys conducted by the Association of American Medical Colleges (AAMC) indicated that by 1987 over 50 percent of medical schools had a nontenure clinician-educator pathway (Moy and others, 1997), and that by 1997 almost 75 percent of schools had either a separate promotion track or specific promotion criteria (Levinson, Branch, and Kroenke, 1998).

During the 1980s a system called cross-subsidization developed. AMCs became increasingly reliant on clinical revenues, generated in large part by these new clinician-educators. These funds were (and still are) used to support faculty in research and education, in terms of direct research support, protected time, and income subsidization (Griner and Blumenthal, 1998; Heinig, Quon, Meyer, and Korn, 1999; Inglehart, 1995; Jones and Sanderson, 1996; Kassirer, 1994; Moy and others, 1997). Comparing the relative growth in the contribution of clinical revenues to overall medical school revenues, the potential problem is obvious. Revenues have increased from 12.1 percent in 1976 to 48.4 percent in 1996 (Jolly and Hudley, 1998). It is estimated that in 1992–93 faculty practice plans subsidized research at a level of $815 million, undergraduate education at $702 million, and graduate medical education at $594 million (Jones and Sanderson, 1996). Cross-subsidization made AMCs and their faculty very vulnerable to changes in the business of medicine.

Managed Care Emerges. Into the 1980s all of American medicine, including academic medicine, lived in an era of abundance. Quality rose, expensive diagnostic technologies and treatments were developed, and both doctors and patients became complacent and assured that if they wanted anything done, private or governmental insurance would pay for it. Health care costs began to command a larger and larger percent of the gross national product, moving from 7.1 percent in 1970 to 10.2 percent in 1985 and 13.7 percent in 1994 (Jolly and Hudley, 1998). Thus a situation emerged as "a widening disparity between the seemingly insatiable demands for resources by the medical profession and the willingness of society to supply these resources" (Korn, 1996). Managed care emerged and the climate in academic medicine changed dramatically (Genel and others, 1996; Greisler, 1998; Kassirer, 1994; Korn, 1996; Swick, 1998).

With managed care now the dominant force in the United States, all three missions of AMCs are being threatened (Inglehart, 1995). Many departmental and institutional leaders have responded to financial pressures by increasing the clinical demands on their members (Greisler, 1998). Thus faculty have been forced to increase their work in practice to the detriment of fulfilling the AMCs' missions of teaching and research (Kataria, 1998). Jordan Cohen, M.D., the president of the AAMC, stated that the ability of academic medical centers to continue financing their activities through cross-subsidization is "problematic in the extreme" (Inglehart, 1995). Academic medicine is in turmoil. No new paradigms have emerged. Both faculty satisfaction and faculty productivity have been negatively impacted.

Models for Examination of Faculty Satisfaction and Faculty Work

Our thorough examination of the literature clearly revealed the need for a comprehensive model to clarify academic medical faculty satisfaction. In response we offer Figure 3.1 that combines elements from the Society of General Internal Medicine's (SGIM) model for physician satisfaction (Gerrity and others, 1997) and Blackburn and Lawrence's (1995) model of faculty work. The authors of the SGIM model postulated that three elements—job characteristics, personal and family characteristics, and community characteristics—interact and result in job-career satisfaction and personal-life satisfaction for practicing physicians. They further hypothesized that job-career satisfaction and personal-life satisfaction interrelate and affect three outcomes: (1) retention in job, specialty, and medicine; (2) quality of patient care; and (3) patient satisfaction.

The Blackburn and Lawrence (1995) model of faculty work was based on a study of university faculty characteristics and their work. The study found that self- and social knowledge can affect behavior and productivity. Self-knowledge included self-efficacy, interest, preferred effort, empowerment, and personal ambition. Social knowledge was composed of institutional support and the effort that faculty believe their institution desires.

Figure 3.1. Suggested Model for Faculty Satisfaction

The three exogenous elements of Figure 3.1 (organizational factors, job-related factors, and personal factors) originated from the faculty satisfaction literature within academic medicine. Next, based on motivational theory and Blackburn and Lawrence's (1995) work, we hypothesize that these factors lead to faculty self-knowledge, social knowledge, and job satisfaction. Finally, the model hypothesizes that positive outcomes such as increased faculty productivity, faculty retention, and patient and learner satisfaction may result.

Outcomes of Faculty Effort. Table 3.1 provides a succinct list of the outcomes identified with medical faculty satisfaction. Three of the studies examined research-related outcomes. Campbell, Weissman, and Blumenthal (1997) found that in medical schools located in areas of high managed care penetration, the number of faculty publications had decreased in comparison to the number at medical schools in low penetration areas. Moy and others (1997) discovered that the number of grant applications, number of grants awarded, and total amount of National Institutes of Health grant funding in those areas had also decreased in comparison to other medical schools. Rosenberg (1999) found that the overall number of physician-submitted applications for basic research funding has decreased at a very rapid rate. Fried (1996) found that the reason most commonly stated by faculty for delays in their career was demoralization, indicating that satisfaction or dissatisfaction may play a role in productivity.

Factors That Affect Faculty Satisfaction. From an examination of a combination of anecdotal and research literature we have classified the components of faculty satisfaction into three categories: (1) organizational factors, (2) job-related factors, and (3) personal factors. In Table 3.2 we list studies conducted on the satisfaction of medical faculty as indexed by the factors of Figure 3.1.

Organizational Factors. Organizational factors relate to the institutional environments in which faculty work. Important organizational factors include: resources available to faculty; perceived opportunities for promotion or advancement; adequacy of mentoring for junior faculty; gender-

Table 3.1. Outcomes Potentially Affected by Faculty Satisfaction

Potential Outcome	*Studies*
Learner perception of teaching quality	Probst, 1998
Patient satisfaction	Atkins, 1996; Osteroff, 1992
Intention to leave or stay at institution	Fried, 1996; Anderson, 1995
Number of faculty publications	Campbell, 1997
Number or dollar amount of National Institutes of Health (NIH) grants	Moy, 1997
Number of NIH grant applications	Rosenberg, 1999

Note: First author and year are listed for each study.

Table 3.2. Factors Affecting Satisfaction

Factors Affecting Faculty Satisfaction	Studies Assessing These Factors
Organizational Factors	
Resources available to faculty	Linn, 1985; Kaplan, 1996; Carr, 1998
Perceived opportunities for promotion	Linn, 1985; Linn, 1986
Adequacy of mentoring	Kaplan, 1996; Fried, 1996
Gender-based obstacles to success	Fried, 1996; Cook, 1995; Fried, 1996; Kaplan, 1996
Appreciation by colleagues	Cook, 1995; Fried, 1996; Levinson, 1993
Collegial relations in department	Campbell, 1997; Simon, 1999; Woodward, 1999 or institution
Role in decision making or ability to have an impact	Linn, 1985; Anderson, 1995
Commitment to the organization	Probst, 1998; Woodward, 1999
Job-Related Factors	
Autonomy or clinical freedom	Schultz, 1992; Probst, 1998
Stimulating work	Linn, 1985; Fried, 1996
Clear and consistent job duties	Anderson, 1995; Woodward, 1999
Gratification from patient care	Linn, 1985; Woods, 1997
Gratification from teaching	Kirz, 1986; Greer, 1990; Levinson, 1993; Garr, 1986; Cook, 1995; Foley, 1996; Woods, 1997
Availability of time and funds for research	Garr, 1986; Cook, 1995; Campbell, 1997; Woods, 1997; Simon, 1999
Work-related time pressures	Linn, 1985; Anderson, 1995; Woodward, 1999
Heavy workload	Losek, 1994; Zinn, 1998
Salary, income	Schultz, 1992; Linn, 1985; Linn, 1986; Woods, 1997; Simon, 1999
Job security	Simon, 1999; Woodward, 1999
Personal Factors	
Perceptions of role conflict	Linn, 1985; Anderson, 1995
Interference of work responsibilities with home	Linn, 1985; Linn, 1986; Losek, 1994; Anderson, 1995; Cook, 1995; Woodward, 1999
Interference of family or other external obligations with work	Linn, 1985; Linn, 1986; Carr, 1998; Woodward, 1999

Note: First author and year are listed for each study.

based obstacles to success; appreciation or respect by colleagues; collegial relations among faculty and staff; faculty role in decision making or the perceived ability to have an impact on the unit or organization; and commitment to the organization. All of these factors contribute to satisfaction when positive (Probst and others, 1998) or are potential sources of dissatisfaction when perceived less positively (Levinson, Kaufman, and Bickel, 1993).

Today, the majority of the anecdotal evidence points to a decrement in the institutional environment of academic medicine (Souba and others,

1995; Moy and others, 1997; Thompson and Moskowitz, 1997; Greisler, 1998; Rosenberg, 1999). The data from research concerning the impact of managed care supports this contention (Campbell and others, 1997). Simon and others (1999) conducted a systematic telephone survey of medical students, residents, faculty, and deans at U.S. medical schools to determine their experiences in and perspectives toward managed care. The attitudes of all respondents toward managed care were overwhelmingly negative. Interestingly, both faculty and deans felt that collegial relations among faculty suffered in the managed care environment.

Virtually all AMCs have gone through dramatic change in response to financial pressures. The only structured study of an AMC in transition (Woodward and others, 1999) found significant changes in staff composition (both medical and nonmedical) as well as in attitudes and perceptions of the job and institution. They found that staff reported not only significant increases in depression, anxiety, and emotional exhaustion but also significant decreases in the ratings of coworker support, supervisor support, teamwork, the overall hospital work environment, and the medical center as an employer.

The data on organizational factors also points out a clear gender difference in perceptions with respect to the institutional environment. All four studies which included comparisons by gender found more negative feelings and lower faculty satisfaction among women faculty (Cook, Griffith, and Sackett, 1995; Fried and others, 1996; Kaplan and others, 1996; Carr and others, 1998). Women reported receiving significantly less institutional support (research support and clerical support) and perceived a wide variety of impediments to career success including lack of effective mentoring, gender bias in promotion and compensation, trouble forming collaborative arrangements, and networking. Women felt much more isolated than men, less welcomed, less supported, and more often denigrated by male colleagues.

Job-Related Factors. Job-related factors relate to the specific elements of an individual faculty member's job. The important factors include (1) autonomy and clinical freedom; (2) stimulation from work; (3) clear and consistent job duties; (4) gratification from teaching and patient care; (5) availability of time and funds for research; (6) work-related time pressures and workload; and (7) income and job security. Most of these factors can contribute to satisfaction when positive (Schultz, Girard, and Scheckler, 1992; Probst and others, 1998) or be a potential source of dissatisfaction when perceived less positively (Losek, 1994; Zinn, Block, and Clark-Chiarelli, 1998).

Numerous studies found that clinical faculty rated teaching as the most satisfying activity and efforts related to research as least satisfying (Kirz and Larsen, 1986; Greer, 1990; Levinson, Kaufman, and Bickel, 1993; Garr, 1986; Anderson and Mavis, 1995; Cook, Griffith, and Sackett, 1995; Foley and others, 1996; Woods and others, 1997). When teaching itself was the focus, the intrinsic rewards of working with students and residents provided the greatest satisfaction, while the need for recognition (financial or other) was the element most needing improvement (Linn and others, 1986; Cook, Griffith, and Sackett, 1995; Woods and others, 1997). Comparing faculty at AMCs with community-based faculty, academic faculty were more concerned with time pressures and less satisfied with their finances (Linn, Yager, Cope, and Leake, 1985).

As with organizational factors, research on the impact of managed care supports that it has changed faculty work. Every recent study that included how faculty spend their time indicated that faculty perceive they now have less time for both research and teaching (Cook, Griffith, and Sackett, 1995; Campbell, Weissman, and Blumenthal, 1997; Woods and others, 1997; Simon and others, 1999). Under managed care, faculty also reported decreased income and job security and increased time pressures (Campbell, Weissman, and Blumenthal, 1997; Simon and others, 1999; Woodward and others, 1999).

Personal Factors. Personal factors connect the job and the faculty member's outside life. Important personal factors include perceptions of role conflict; interference of work responsibilities with home, family, or other external activities; and interference of family or other external obligations with work. In the studies of the impact of managed care, only Woodward and others (1999) examined personal factors. In their examination of an AMC during reengineering, they found that staff reported both an increase in work interfering with home life, and to a lesser extent outside demands interfering with work.

Summary and Suggestions

Academic medicine is in turmoil; this indicates the need for consistent and ongoing research in faculty satisfaction. The model proposed herein contains many areas examined only sparsely. Evidence shows that changes in AMCs resulting from the advent of managed care (and other cost-cutting measures) impact all three areas of faculty satisfaction: organizational, job-related, and personal. There is also evidence that satisfaction is related to outcomes such as learner perceptions of teaching quality (see Table 3.1). Thus, the groundwork has been laid, but there is much work still to be done.

Due to recent radical and stressful changes, academic medical faculty roles have altered, giving way to increased emphasis on generating clinical income accompanied by fewer resources for teaching and research. Medical schools and AMCs should be aware of the impact of change on faculty satisfaction. Faculty in these difficult times are encouraged to be "clear-eyed, responsive, and innovative and to never give up" (Rabkin, 1998, p. 127). But they cannot do this alone. There is much that AMCs can do to support faculty during the paradigm shift (Kataria, 1998). The literature on faculty satisfaction can provide insight and guidance into that process.

References

Anderson, K. D., and Mavis, B. E. "The Relationship Between Career Satisfaction and Fellowship Training in Academic Surgeons." *American Journal of Surgery,* 1995, *169,* 329–333.

Atkins, P. M., Marshall, B. S., and Javalgi, R. G. "Happy Employees Lead to Loyal Patients." *Journal of Health Care Marketing,* 1996, *16,* 15–23.

Blackburn, R. T., and Lawrence, J. H. *Faculty at Work: Motivation, Expectation and Satisfaction.* Baltimore: Johns Hopkins University Press, 1995.

Burrow, G. N. "Tensions Within the Academic Health Center." *Academic Medicine,* 1993, *68,* 585–587.

Campbell, E. G., Weissman, J. S., and Blumenthal, D. "Relationship Between Market Competition and the Activities and Attitudes of Medical School Faculty." *Journal of the American Medical Association,* 1997, *278,* 222–226.

Carr, P. L., and others. "Relation of Family Responsibilities and Gender to the Productivity and Career Satisfaction of Medical Family." *Annals of Internal Medicine,* 1998, *129*(7), 532–538.

Cook, D. J., Griffith, L. E., and Sackett, D. L. "Importance of and Satisfaction with Work and Professional Interpersonal Issues: A Survey of Physicians Practicing General Internal Medicine in Ontario." *Canadian Medical Association Journal,* 1995, *153*(6), 755–764.

Foley, R., and others. "Recruiting and Retaining Volunteer Preceptors." *Academic Medicine,* 1996, *71,* 460–463.

Fried, L. P., and others. "Career Development for Women in Academic Medicine: Multiple Interventions in a Department of Medicine." *Journal of the American Medical Association,* 1996, *276*(11), 898–905.

Garr, D. R. "Characteristics and Job Satisfaction of Family Physicians in Full-Time Teaching." *Family Medicine,* 1986, *18,* 269–273.

Genel, M., and others. "1995 Public Policy Plenary Symposium: 'The Crisis in Clinical Research.'" *Pediatric Research,* 1996, *39*(5), 902–913.

Gerrity, M. S., and others. "Career Satisfaction and Clinician-Educators." *Journal of General Internal Medicine,* 1997, *12*(Supplement 2), S90-S97.

Greer, D. S. "Faculty Rewards for the Generalist Clinician-Teacher." *Journal of General Internal Medicine,* 1990, *5*(Supplement 1), S53-S58.

Greisler, H. P. "Presidential Address: The Hour Is Getting Late." *Journal of Vascular Surgery,* 1998, *27*(5), 795–804.

Griner, P. F., and Blumenthal, D. "New Bottles for Vintage Wines: The Changing Management of the Medical School Faculty." *Academic Medicine,* 1998, *73*(6), 719–724.

Heinig, S. J., Quon, A.S.W., Meyer, R. E., and Korn, D. "The Changing Landscape for Clinical Research." *Academic Medicine,* 1999, *74*(6), 725–745.

Inglehart, J. K. "Rapid Changes for Academic Medical Centers (Second of Two Parts)." *New England Journal of Medicine,* 1995, *332*(6), 407–411.

Jolly, P., and Hudley, D. M. (eds.). *AAMC Data Book: Statistical Information Related to Medical Education.* Washington, D.C.: Association of American Medical Colleges, 1998.

Jones, R. F., and Sanderson, S. C. "Clinical Revenues Used to Support the Academic Mission of Medical Schools, 1992–3." *Academic Medicine,* 1996, *71*(3), 299–307.

Kaplan, S. H., and others. "Sex Differences in Academic Advancement—Results of a National Study of Pediatricians." *New England Journal of Medicine,* 1996, *335*(17), 1282–1289.

Kassirer, J. P. "Academic Medical Centers Under Siege." *New England Journal of Medicine,* 1994, *331*(20), 1370–1371.

Kataria, S. "The Turmoil of Academic Physicians: What AMCs Can Do to Ease the Pain." *Academic Medicine,* 1998, *73*(7), 728–730.

Kirz, H. L., and Larsen, C. "Costs and Benefits of Medical Student Training to Health Organizations." *Journal of the American Medical Association*, 1986, *18*, 269–273.

Korn, D. "Reengineering Academic Medical Centers: Reengineering Academic Values?" *Academic Medicine*, 1996, *71*(2), 1033–1043.

Levinson, W., Branch, W. T., Jr., and Kroenke, K. "Clinician-Educators in Academic Medical Centers: A Two-Part Challenge." *Annals of Internal Medicine*, 1998, *129*(1), 59–64.

Levinson, W., Kaufman, K., and Bickel, J. "Part-Time Faculty in Academic Medicine: Present Status and Future Challenges." *Annals of Internal Medicine*, 1993, *119*(3), 220–225.

Levinson, W., and Rubenstein, A. "Integrating Clinician-Educators into Academic Medical Centers." *New England Journal of Medicine*, 1999, *341*(11), 840–844.

Linn, L. S., Yager, J., Cope, D., and Leake, B. "Health Status, Job Satisfaction, Job Stress, and Life Satisfaction Among Academic and Clinical Faculty." *Journal of the American Medical Association*, 1985, *254*(19), 2775–2782.

Linn, L. S., and others. "Work Satisfaction and Career Aspirations of Internists Working in Teaching Hospital Group Practices." *Journal of General Internal Medicine*, 1986, *1*, 104–108.

Losek, J. D. "Characteristics, Workload, and Job Satisfaction of Attending Physicians from Pediatric Emergency Medicine Fellowship Programs." *Pediatric Emergency Care*, 1994, *10*(5), 256–259.

Moy, E., and others. "Relationship Between National Institutes of Health Research Awards to U.S. Medical Schools and Managed Care Market Penetration." *Journal of the American Medical Association*, 1997, *278*(3), 217–221.

Osteroff, C. "The Relationship Between Satisfaction, Attitudes, and Performance: An Organizational Level Analysis." *Journal of Applied Psychology*, 1992, *77*, 963–974.

Pardes, H. "The Future of Medical Schools and Teaching Hospitals in the Era of Managed Care." *Academic Medicine*, 1997, *72*(2), 97–102.

Probst, J. C., and others. "Organizational Environment and Perceptions of Teaching Quality in Seven South Carolina Family Medicine Residency Programs." *Academic Medicine*, 1998, *73*(8), 887–893.

Rabkin, M. T. "A Paradigm Shift in Academic Medicine?" *Academic Medicine*, 1998, *73*(2), 127–131.

Rosenberg, L. E. "Physician-Scientists: Endangered and Essential." *Science*, 1999, *283*, 331–332.

Schultz, R., Girard, C., and Scheckler, W. E. "Physician Satisfaction in a Managed Care Environment." *Journal of Family Practice*, 1992, *34*(2), 298–304.

Simon, S. R., and others. "Views of Managed Care—A Survey of Students, Residents, Faculty, and Deans at Medical Schools in the United States." *New England Journal of Medicine*, 1999, *340*(12), 928–936.

Souba, W. W., and others. "Strategies for Success in Academic Surgery." *Surgery*, 1995, *117*, 90–95.

Swick, H. M. "Academic Medicine Must Deal with the Clash of Business and Professional Values." *Academic Medicine*, 1998, *73*(7), 751–755.

Thompson, J. N., and Moskowitz, J. "Preventing the Extinction of the Clinical Research Ecosystem." *Journal of the American Medical Association*, 1997, *278*(3), 241–245.

Woods, S. E., and others. "Collegial Networking and Faculty Vitality." *Family Medicine*, 1997, *29*(1), 45–49.

Woodward, C. A., and others. "The Impact of Re-Engineering and Other Cost Reduction Strategies on the Staff of a Large Teaching Hospital: A Longitudinal Study." *Medical Care*, 1999, *37*(6), 556–569.

Zinn, W. M., Block, S. D., and Clark-Chiarelli, N. "Enthusiasm for Primary Care: Comparing Family Medicine and General Internal Medicine." *Journal of General Internal Medicine*, 1998, *13*(3), 186–194.

JULIE G. NYQUIST is professor in the Division of Medical Education, University of Southern California.

MAURICE A. HITCHCOCK is professor of education and pediatrics and director of the Division of Medical Education, University of Southern California.

ARIANNE TEHERANI is research associate in the Division of Medical Education, University of Southern California.

4

With a special look at the experience of several community college locals in California, this chapter explores faculty satisfaction with unionization and considers the implications for the future role of the faculty union.

Community College Faculty Satisfaction and the Faculty Union

Consuelo Rey Castro '

Over the past thirty-five years, community colleges in the United States have experienced a multitude of changes that mirror changes taking place in society. Kerchner, Koppich, and Weeres (1997) describe this change as a "transformation—a major shifting of the tectonic plates underlying the institutions of public education" (p. 5). Some of the grandest traditions of higher education are grudgingly making room for what is new while others just fade away. The decline of tenured faculty with increasing reliance on part-time faculty is a prime example. But there are others. Technology continues to transform the curriculum and our classrooms. Nontraditional students, often underprepared, are fast becoming the new student majority at community colleges. With public support, legislative leaders are increasingly linking higher education funding to reform movement initiatives meant to restore quality in undergraduate education. These ongoing changes and many others continue to spark controversy, meet with resistance, and create conflict. They continue to have their greatest impact on the working conditions and professional lives of the faculty. Partly in response to these changes that may be perceived to challenge job security and satisfaction among college teachers, faculty turned to unionization (Kemerer and Baldridge, 1975; Kerchner and Mitchell, 1988; Rhoades, 1998).

The faculty union, traceable to the old industrial order, is not immune to the changes taking place in higher education (Kerchner and Mitchell, 1988; Kerchner, Koppich, and Weeres, 1997; Rhoades, 1998). Educators, policy makers, researchers, union leaders, and faculty would all benefit from a better understanding of how these changes are affecting faculty satisfaction.

This chapter explores the experience of several community college faculty unions in California. The following research questions are addressed: (1) What contemporary factors of change contribute to faculty satisfaction and dissatisfaction with unionization? (2) How has the faculty union responded to these change factors and to changes in faculty satisfaction? (3) What are the implications for faculty satisfaction and the role of the faculty union?

A number of early studies are included along with the more recent literature to provide an understanding of the political and economic context of collective bargaining as well as to compare contemporary with traditional change factors. Many recent studies examine the ongoing effects of unionization on faculty satisfaction by looking at compensation and governance. Expanding outside these traditional areas however, is a growing body of literature about the role of the faculty union, particularly in the area of education reform. The consequences of unionization go well beyond faculty satisfaction, job security, compensation, and working conditions, extending to educational policy and outcomes. Faculty unions are under pressure to take responsibility for faculty work–teaching and learning (Kerchner and Mitchell, 1988; Kerchner, Koppich, and Weeres, 1997; Timpane and White, 1998; Colvin, 1999).

Although the literature looks at various dimensions of faculty satisfaction and unionization in higher education, little research about this important phenomenon at two-year colleges exists. Given the scope and density of unionization at the community college level (Cohen and Brawer, 1996; Rhoades, 1998; Aronowitz, 1998b), I hope that the questions raised in this chapter will serve as an impetus for additional research.

Collective Bargaining in Higher Education

Unions began to organize faculty in higher education with the passage of federal and state legislation expanding collective bargaining to public employees in the 1960s. The three major unions representing college and university faculty are the American Federation of Teachers, the Association of American University Professors, and the National Education Association (NEA). The first faculty units unionized in 1965 at two community colleges in Michigan (Cameron, 1982). By 1994, 44 percent of full-time faculty (or 242,221 faculty on 1,057 campuses) were represented by bargaining agents. The heaviest concentration of unionization occurred in the public sector: 60 percent of colleges and universities and 63 percent of the full-time faculty (Rhoades, 1998). Today, the public community colleges have the highest concentration of union representation at 94 percent (or 103,967 faculty). As a result, unionization in higher education is often perceived as a community college phenomenon (Wiley, 1993). In a nationwide study, Rhoades (1998) reported that statewide systems of colleges and universities have the highest total number (138,254) of unionized faculty.

In California, the passage of the 1976 Rodda Act authorized collective bargaining for public sector employees. It limited the scope of bargaining to three-year contracts covering salary, working conditions, and procedures for termination and reduction in force (Rubiales, 1998). Two years after it was established, "40 percent of the community college districts were unionized" (Wiley, 1993, p. 158). Today, "all but one" of California's 107 community colleges is unionized (Rubiales, p. 40). In practice, negotiated contracts are not limited to compensation, working conditions, and job security issues, they also address personnel policies, governance, and academic issues (Kerchner and Mitchell, 1988; Cohen and Brawer, 1996; Kerchner, Koppich, and Weeres, 1997).

Faculty Satisfaction/Dissatisfaction Factors and Unionization

Faculty dissatisfaction with job security, compensation, and governance issues provided the historical impetus for collective bargaining in higher education. Yet contemporary education reform efforts present a growing challenge to faculty satisfaction with unionization.

Historical Context. The 1960s and 1970s were the initial period in which political and economic events most adversely impacted the compensation and working conditions of faculty (Kemerer and Baldridge, 1975). Inflation coupled with prolonged recession, declining student enrollments, increased education costs, diminishing public support, and cuts in education funding all contributed to undermining faculty working conditions, job security, and morale (Feuille and Blandin, 1974; Kemerer and Baldridge, 1975; Lussier, 1975). Other issues contributing to community college faculty dissatisfaction were: heavy teaching loads, large classes, underprepared students, low compensation, lack of support, bureaucracy, and administration (Keim, 1988; Milosheff, 1990). The implementation of "new management techniques . . . within fiscal constraints" created greater faculty distrust and declining satisfaction with working conditions (Kemerer and Baldridge, p. 46). Collective bargaining became the vehicle for addressing that dissatisfaction.

Faculty Dissatisfaction Factors and Unionization. Job security, compensation, and working conditions were the areas of faculty dissatisfaction most cited for contract negotiations (Feuille and Blandin, 1974; Kemerer and Baldridge, 1975; Kerchner and Mitchell, 1988). Community colleges with lower-income students and weak governance processes were most favorable to unionization (Feuille and Blandin, 1974; Kemerer and Baldridge, 1975; Kerchner and Mitchell, 1988). A recent study of the reasons faculty supported collective bargaining reported "both specific and overall job satisfaction are inversely correlated with attitudes toward unionization and with a pro-union vote" (Graf, Hemmasi, Newgren, and Nielsen, 1994, p. 153). In other words, as job satisfaction declined, attitudes supporting unionization increased. "The link is clear—the lower the satisfaction with working conditions, the higher the desire for unionization" (Kemerer and Baldridge, 1975, p. 64).

The recognition that "academic issues represent the areas in which unions will continue to extend their contractual influence" (Graf, Hemmasi, Newgren, and Nielsen, 1994, p. 152) suggests that colleges with weak and ineffective governance structures—traditionally responsible for making policy in academic areas—would increasingly move toward collective bargaining (Drummond and Reitsch, 1995).

Unionization's Impact on Governance. When the traditional collegial model of governance was replaced with an "industrial model," administration essentially gained power "at the faculty's expense" while faculty relations with administration shifted to that of an employee with employer (Crossland, 1976, p. 42). Thus, the view of the contract limiting the "arbitrary exercise of power by administrators" underscores the role of the faculty union in providing faculty satisfaction through empowerment (p. 42). In restoring the faculty's governance role, collective bargaining functioned as a countervailing force (Dennison, Drummond, and Hobgood, 1997). The effects of unionization on governance have been strongest where governance processes were weak, and minimal where strong faculty senates were in place (Kemerer and Baldridge, 1975; Crossland, 1976; Lee, 1979; Ponak, Thompson, and Zerbe, 1992; Drummond and Reitsch, 1995).

The American Council on Education, the Association of Governing Boards of Universities and Colleges, and the Association of American University Professors (1987) confirmed in a joint statement that unionization complemented and supported faculty governance, particularly on campuses where "problems in institutional governance [contributed] to the emergence of collective bargaining" (p. 25). Institutions that had strong shared governance structures and processes before collective bargaining were more likely to maintain effective collegial governance after unionization (Ponak, Thompson, and Zerbe, 1992; Drummond and Reitsch, 1995). And the role of collective bargaining at such institutions was limited to the traditional areas of compensation and working conditions. However, faculty unions at colleges with weak and ineffective governance systems began to address academic and professional matters in addition to traditional concerns. These colleges "tend[ed] to become more embattled and less collegial" (Drummond and Reitsch, p. 56). This increased the likelihood that academic and professional matters were included in the scope of bargaining (Ponak, Thompson, and Zerbe, 1992; Drummond and Reitsch, 1995). Collective bargaining became a variant of governance, albeit "an extreme form of shared governance, wherein the rules are legally rather than collegially established" (Drummond and Reitsch, p. 57). Several interesting conclusions emerge from these studies. Strong faculty governance systems can successfully coexist with unionization; and, where governance is weak, faculty unions have a tendency to address academic and professional matters at the bargaining table (Ponak, Thompson, and Zerbe, 1992; Drummond and Reitsch, 1995; Dennison, Drummond, and Hobgood, 1997). Thus it seems the faculty union has positively contributed to faculty satisfaction in the area of governance.

Unionization's Impact on Compensation. While the influence of collective bargaining on salary and benefits has fluctuated, faculty satisfaction with unionization on compensation has remained stable. Morgan and Kearney (1977) compared salaries over two bargaining periods at forty-six union and nonunion baccalaureate institutions and found that unionized faculty earned an average of one thousand dollars more than nonunion faculty. They concluded that the union variable was the most significant factor in explaining faculty satisfaction with salary. Two years later in a similar study, Marshall (1979) found "little, if any difference" in compensation levels between union and nonunion faculty (p. 318). He concluded that while unionization initially increased faculty salaries, these gains "were not sustained over the long term" (p. 311). Gomez-Mejia and Balkin (1984) compared the effects of unionization on faculty satisfaction with compensation and other dimensions of pay at unionized and nonunionized multicampus university systems. They found that unionized faculty were more satisfied with both the economic and noneconomic aspects of their jobs.

A study by Finley (1991) on faculty satisfaction levels at public two-year colleges in nineteen Midwestern states found that although unionized faculty had lower mean salaries than their nonunionized counterparts, they still indicated moderate levels of satisfaction (p. 58). Wiley (1993) found that collective bargaining at California's community colleges initially increased compensation but failed to "have a significant, positive effect on salary over time" (p. 170). Community college faculty have benefited from unionization "although not nearly as much as its proponents had hoped or as much as its detractors had feared" (Cohen and Brawer, 1996, p. 75). These findings and others strongly indicate that although compensation may contribute to faculty satisfaction, it has not been the primary factor contributing to satisfaction with the faculty union (Aronowitz, 1998a, 1998b).

The Changing Role of the Faculty Union

Kerchner and Koppich (1993) distinguished between two models of faculty unionism: industrial unionism and professional unionism. In industrial unionism, the primary emphasis is protecting employees—job security. In contrast, professional unionism emphasizes academic values. Industrial unionism's rule-bound procedures and contractual agreements have contributed to adversarial relations, greater centralization of power, and the growth of burgeoning bureaucratization (Kemerer and Baldridge, 1975; Kerchner and Mitchell, 1988; Kerchner and Koppich, 1993). In particular, teaching assignments based on industrial-style seniority rules instead of merit have often worked to undermine quality education and adversely affect student performance outcomes (Kerchner and Mitchell, 1988; Kerchner and Koppich, 1993; Aronowitz, 1998a, 1998b). The quality of higher education at unionized institutions depends on whether or not faculty union leaders assume the role of professional unionism (Kemerer and Baldridge, 1975; Kerchner and Mitchell, 1988; Kerchner, Koppich, and Weeres, 1997). "The transition from one generation [industrial unionism] to the next generation [professional unionism] begins with the accumulation of dissatisfaction over the established mode of unionization and an impetus toward reform" (Kerchner and Mitchell, 1988, pp. 13–14). By addressing teaching and learning, professional unionism successfully combines faculty interest with public interest (Kerchner and Mitchell, 1988; Kerchner and Koppich, 1993, Kerchner, Koppich, and Weeres, 1997). The dynamics involved in the transition have major implications for faculty satisfaction, particularly at community colleges.

The View of Faculty Union Presidents

During the spring of 1999, I invited the presidents of six California community college faculty unions to participate in individual interviews. The interviews had a dual purpose: (1) to identify current factors influencing faculty satisfaction with unionization and (2) to query this elite group regarding present changes in their unions. Four presidents responded and two of the union locals were chosen for follow-up in the fall of 1999. The four colleges are described as:

Faculty Union	College District
Promise	Multicollege (urban and suburban)
Vigilance	Multicollege (suburban)
Enigma	Single-college (urban)
Common Good	Single-college (suburban)

Community College Faculty Union Experiences

Overall findings from the interviews indicated that single-college unions may be more successful at attaining greater faculty satisfaction than multicollege unions. Both Promise and Vigilance described faculty as "generally" and "relatively" satisfied with the union; both Enigma and Common Good described their faculty as "very satisfied" and "satisfied." This difference may be unique to these particular faculty unions or it may reflect a consistent distinction between single and multicollege unions.

Representation. The most important factor contributing to faculty satisfaction at both Promise and Vigilance was "strong" and "vigorous" representation. While both Enigma and Common Good also provide representation, neither identified it as a primary factor contributing to faculty satisfaction. Common Good explained that they deal with problems through faculty teamwork. "This really contributes to faculty satisfaction in our local." It also points to a collegial work environment in which faculty are engaged in working together toward common goals.

Compensation. Historically, low salaries have served as a source of faculty dissatisfaction at Promise. But a contract settlement several years ago resulted in the biggest salary boost in the history of the local. This "salary increase contributed to greater faculty satisfaction and a renewed respect among faculty for the work of the union." Faculty satisfaction with compensation has consistently been strong at Vigilance and Common Good, where salaries are well above the state average. "Faculty credit regular salary increases to the hard work of the union."

Educational Reform. The responses to this contemporary change factor reflected a realignment of the four unions. Both Promise (multicollege) and Common Good (single-college) expressed strong support for a union role in education reform; both Vigilance (multicollege) and Enigma (single-colleges) expressed strong to moderate opposition. The president at Promise believes that, "despite the legal assignment of academic and professional matters to Academic Senates by AB1725 (the California community college reform bill), the faculty union should whenever possible be a leader of educational reform." The president of Common Good stated that, "We should be in the forefront of supporting quality education and always remember that we sought to work in public education to serve the public."

In contrast, the president at Vigilance responded that the "only role of the union in educational reform is to protect the rights of union members. The union cannot trust administration and should not collaborate with them on educational reform because management can manipulate the process to weaken the union." This industrial unionism response reflects distrust and suspicion of administration.

When asked how faculty would respond if the union took a leadership role in supporting reform issues, both Promise and Enigma cautiously responded that it would depend on the specific reform and how faculty perceived it affecting them. They both agreed that reforms from outside the district would generally meet with resistance and faculty dissatisfaction, especially reforms targeting teaching and learning or student-based outcomes such as retention and transfer. Faculty union activists at Promise are very divided about the appropriateness of the union's involvement in reform, particularly when it challenges job security provisions like seniority and evaluation—integral units of industrial unionism. At Vigilance, adversarial relations with the administration obstruct any real consideration by the union of a role in reform: "if taking a role in supporting educational reform meant the union leadership had to work with the administration, the membership would revolt . . . they would never accept it."

Campus Climate. Following are two cases that illustrate how campus climate affects the roles of unions.

Common Good: Professional Unionism at Work. Common Good, a single-college district, is located in a suburban middle-class neighborhood. The union president indicated that the college has been publicly committed to academic as well as employment issues for some time. This founding commitment to balance academic quality with traditional union concerns of compensation and working conditions reflects values that evolved alongside strong governance structures already in place. Not surprisingly, the union president advocates professional unionism and believes that Common Good is a model of professional unionism at work. The culture of the organization, not just its structure, is committed to education and to effectively serving students. The contract provides excellent salaries (in the top third statewide) and working conditions and is designed to ensure that student and departmental needs are also met. Faculty are required to work on campus at least thirty hours per week. And although faculty are provided job security and rights to representation, a rigorous peer evaluation process permits the union and administration to protect students from bad teachers. The union president admitted that over the years, the union has on occasion carefully and discreetly helped faculty to retire when they deserved to be terminated. At other times, the union has pressured the administration to use the contract to hold certain faculty accountable, especially when there is evidence that they may not be good for students.

A visit to the campus and observation of a faculty meeting confirmed that practice at Common Good reflects the ideals of professional unionism. The faculty union and the academic senate not only share the same office and secretary, they also share responsibility for the academic quality of educational programs. Collegial working relationships with the administration are based on mutual respect and trust. Although consultation with the college president takes place on a weekly basis, both presidents maintain an open door policy with each other to facilitate effective communication. Even the union's monthly newsletter reflects these ideals. It includes a regular column for the union president, the academic senate president, the classified council, the adjunct faculty, a faculty profile, and several articles about effective teaching and professional development opportunities.

Promise: Industrial Unionism Undergoing Change. Promise is a multi-college union in a large metropolitan city representing faculty at colleges in poor and working-class urban neighborhoods and middle-class suburban communities. Historically, union leaders at Promise have proudly regarded their contract as a model emulated by other faculty unions. It reflected political clout in supporting winning candidates for the local governing board, prowess at the bargaining table, and commitment to protecting faculty rights. Crafted in the mid-1970s, it is a basic industrial job protection contract with strong seniority and weak evaluation provisions.

Over the years both the union and administration have invested enormous time and resources interpreting and enforcing the elaborately detailed rules and procedures. Even as college presidents and faculty leaders complained about losing authority to make decisions at the campus level, centralization continued at the district office. Generally satisfied with the employment protection the contract provided, faculty grew dissatisfied in as many years with low salaries, poor working conditions, and high union dues. Other than an initial boost in salary during the early years of unionization, faculty in Promise have not reaped the rewards of improved working conditions and higher salaries.

The current union president decentralized the district office and improved salaries during his first term in office, greatly contributing to faculty satisfaction. He stated that "we are accustomed to adversarial relations with management and criticism from the press. What has emerged over the past several years is a particularly troublesome split amongst the union leadership about the role of our union." By advocating reform of the contract, the negotiations team apparently brought this conflict to the surface. After meeting with faculty at each of the colleges and discussing current needs, they proposed changing the evaluation and seniority provisions in order to improve quality academic services to students. Old-guard leaders on the union's governing council were outraged. They argued that the negotiating team sounded "like a bunch of anti-union administrators" and that the union's only responsibility was to protect faculty jobs. A two-term member of the governing council put it this way: "debate about the proposed reforms was occasionally profound, but mostly it was heated and angry; insults and accusations flew across the room. It was obvious that old-guard leaders were not interested in rational discussion; their primary objective was to block the proposed changes." In a very close vote reflecting the division of the governing council, proposed reforms to evaluation and seniority provisions were defeated. As it turned out, administration ensured modifications in seniority and evaluation by packaging them at the negotiating table with increases in salary and maintenance of benefits. Knowing that rank-and-file faculty would vote to approve the proposed package without their recommendation, a divided governing council voted to recommend ratification of the tentative contract. This conflict is not just a power struggle between old-guard union leaders trying to maintain the status quo of industrial unionism and reform leadership advocating professional academic unionism. Both the administration and rank-and-file faculty may play a key role in the outcome of this power struggle.

Implications and Conclusion

Expanding outside the traditional areas of job security issues, compensation, and governance is a growing body of literature about how education reform is changing the faculty union's role and faculty satisfaction. The challenge holds that industrial unionization has consequences extending well beyond faculty satisfaction with job security, compensation, and working conditions—consequences that contribute to poor academic practices and outcomes (Rabban, 1992). Faculty unions are under pressure to step up to the plate and take responsibility for their part in the other half of faculty work, teaching and learning (Kerchner and Mitchell, 1988; Kerchner, Koppich, and Weeres, 1997; Colvin, 1999). This projected change in the faculty union's role has major implications for faculty satisfaction.

Educational reform serves as a contemporary change factor that may contribute to either faculty satisfaction or dissatisfaction with unionization. Adversarial relations with administration, strong industrial union values among union leadership, and a culture of faculty insecurity are all conditions that may undermine faculty satisfaction and limit or obstruct the union's role in reform. Conditions that support and facilitate faculty satisfaction with a union's role in reform include leadership, development of collegial relations, education and participation of faculty, and existing faculty satisfaction with representation, compensation, and working conditions. Faculty dissatisfaction ushered in unionization and is contributing to the changing role of the union.

References

American Council on Education, Association of Governing Boards of Universities and Colleges, and Association of American University Professors. "Statement on Academic Government for Institutions Engaged in Collective Bargaining: A Report." *Academe,* 1987, *73*(6), 25–26.

Aronowitz, S. "Are Unions Good for Professors?" *Academe,* 1998a, *84*(6), 12–17.

Aronowitz, S. *From the Ashes of the Old: American Labor and America's Future.* Boston: Houghton Mifflin, 1998b.

Cameron, K. "The Relationship Between Faculty Unionism and Organizational Effectiveness." *Academy of Management Journal,* 1982, *25*(1), 6–24.

Cohen, A. M., and Brawer, F. B. *The American Community College.* (3rd ed.) San Francisco: Jossey-Bass, 1996.

Colvin, R. L. "Selling Teachers on School Reform," *Los Angeles Times,* May 5, 1999.

Crossland, F. E. "Will the Academy Survive Unionization?" *Change,* 1976, *8*(1), 38–42.

Dennison, G. M., Drummond, M. E., and Hobgood, W. P. "Collaborative Bargaining in Public Universities: Case Analysis." *Negotiations Journal,* 1997, *13*(1), 61–81.

Drummond, M. E., and Reitsch, A. "The Relationship Between Shared Governance Models and Faculty and Administrator Attitudes." *Journal of Higher Education Management,* 1995, *11*(1), 49–58.

Feuille, P., and Blandin, J. "Faculty Job Satisfaction and Bargaining Sentiments: A Case Study." *Academy of Management Journal,* 1974, *17*(4), 678–692.

Finley, C. E. "The Relationship Between Unionization and Job Satisfaction Among Two-Year College Faculty." *Community College Review,* 1991, *19*(2), 53–60.

Gomez-Mejia, L. R., and Balkin, D. B. "Faculty Satisfaction with Pay and Other Job Dimensions Under Union and Nonunion Conditions." *Academy of Management Journal,* 1984, *27*(3), 591–602.

Graf, L. A., Hemmasi, M., Newgren, K. E., and Nielsen, W. R. "Profiles of Those Who Support Collective Bargaining in Institutions of Higher Learning and Why." *Journal of Collective Negotiations,* 1994, *23*(2), 151–162.

Keim, M. C. "Two-Year College Faculty: Research Update." *Community College Review,* 1988, *17*(3), 34–43.

Kemerer, F. R., and Baldridge, V. J. *Unions on Campus.* San Francisco: Jossey-Bass, 1975.

Kerchner, C. T., and Koppich, J. E. (eds.). *A Union of Professionals: Labor Relations and Educational Reform.* New York: Teachers College Press, 1993.

Kerchner, C. T., Koppich, J. E., and Weeres, J. G. *United Mind Workers: Unions and Teaching in the Knowledge Society.* San Francisco: Jossey-Bass, 1997.

Kerchner, C. T., and Mitchell, D. E. *The Changing Idea of a Teachers' Union.* Philadelphia: Falmer Press, 1988.

Lee, B. A. "Governance at Unionized Four-Year Colleges: Effect on Decision-Making Structures." *Journal of Higher Education,* 1979, *50*(5), 565–585.

Lussier, V. L. "Faculty Bargaining Associations: National Objectives Versus Campus Contracts." *Journal of Higher Education,* 1975, *46*(5), 507–517.

Marshall, J. L. "The Effects of Collective Bargaining on Faculty Salaries in Higher Education." *Journal of Higher Education,* 1979, *50*(3), 310–322.

Milosheff, E. "Factors Contributing to Job Satisfaction at the Community College." *Community College Review,* 1990, *18*(1), 12–22.

Morgan, D. R., and Kearney, R. C. "Collective Bargaining and Faculty Compensation: A Comparative Analysis." *Sociology of Education,* 1977, *50*(1), 28–39.

Ponak, A., Thompson, M., and Zerbe, W. "Collective Bargaining Goals of University Faculty." *Research in Higher Education,* 1992, *33*(4), 415–431.

Rabban, D. M. "Is Unionization Compatible with Professionalism?" In B. H. Johnson (ed.), *The Impact of Collective Bargaining on Higher Education: A Twenty Year Perspective.* New York: Baruch College, City University of New York, 1992.

Rhoades, G. *Managed Professionals: Unionized Faculty and Restructuring Academic Labor.* New York: State University of New York, 1998.

Rubiales, D. M. "Collective Bargaining at Community Colleges: A Report from California." *Academe,* 1998, *81*(6), 40–42.

Timpane, P. M., and White, L. S. (eds.). *Higher Education and School Reform.* San Francisco: Jossey-Bass, 1998.

Wiley, C. "A Historical Look at the Effect of Collective Bargaining on Faculty Salaries in California Community Colleges." *Journal of Collective Negotiations,* 1993, *22*(2), 157–172.

CONSUELO REY CASTRO is professor of political science and chair of the Social Science Department at East Los Angeles College. A longtime union activist and former chief negotiator for American Federation of Teachers Local 1521, she is also a Ph.D. candidate at the University of Southern California.

5

Although faculty satisfaction is a serious issue for all faculty, the implications specific to faculty of color may be even more intense. This chapter discusses satisfaction among faculty of color, their paths to tenure and promotion, and issues pertaining to job retention.

Job Satisfaction Among Faculty of Color in Academe: Individual Survivors or Institutional Transformers?

Berta Vigil Laden, Linda Serra Hagedorn

> I ask myself . . . what does it mean to be a faculty of color? We are asked to caretake the institution, caretake individuals, while maintaining an excellent research record, integrated with one's teaching portfolio, and carrying the load of at least five faculty members. And given that we are so few, when we do not generate the record, the vita they are able to see, not the one that is an accurate reflection of our daily labor, the problem, mysteriously, becomes fiercely individualized.
> —Gloria Cuádraz (1998, p. 2)

When faculty of color are hired in an institution of higher education, it is not uncommon to find themselves being an "only" in their department or one of a mere two or three "others." Clearly, underrepresented faculty—persons of African American, American Indian, Asian Pacific American, or Latino origin—are a minority presence at most colleges and universities. While the term *minority* conveys smallness in numbers, it may also convey a less positive, and perhaps even a derogatory connotation; hence, the term *faculty of color* is preferred and will be used throughout this chapter.

Most often when faculty of color are hired in academe, only a few enter as tenure-track faculty while many others gain entry through non-tenure-track positions such as lecturer or instructor. As "onlys" or as a few "others" in their institutions, faculty of color often face issues and barriers, such as low to nonexistent social and emotional support and heightened feelings of loneliness and isolation at a level much higher than that experienced by their White counterparts. The essence and definers of job satisfaction may be unique for faculty of color, who are confronted with a significantly more limited opportunity structure.

After a brief introduction, this chapter looks at the following questions: How satisfied are faculty of color in environments where they constitute a minority presence? How do they persevere and survive as individuals to tenure and promotion? Do they leave, prematurely forced out by a nonsupportive atmosphere and less than ideal working environment? And what specific factors contribute to their job satisfaction?

Introduction

One of the most visible and acknowledged demographic changes in higher education since the 1970s has been the increasing racial and ethnic diversity of students; yet this change has not been accompanied by a similarly increasing racial and ethnic diversity of faculty. As Gainen and Boice note, there is "a disturbing flatness in the faculty curve" (1993, p. 1). Although the numbers of faculty people of color have risen, they have not kept pace with their growing numbers in the U.S. population as a whole nor with the increased presence of students of color at the undergraduate level (National Center for Education Statistics, 1999).

By virtue of their minority status, faculty of color experience the academy very differently from nonminority faculty (Johnsrud and Des Jarlais, 1994; Padilla and Chávez, 1995; Turner and Myers, 1999). A literature review by Tack and Patitu (1992) and recent empirical studies (Astin, Antonio, Cress, and Astin, 1997; Johnsrud and Des Jarlais, 1994; Turner and Myers, 1999; Smith, Wolf, and Busenberg, 1996) indicate that most faculty of color experience racial and ethnic bias in the workplace.

How Satisfied Are Faculty of Color in Environments Where They Constitute a Minority Presence?

A recent study by Astin, Antonio, Cress, and Astin (1997) using national data from 1995–1996 of 33,986 full-time college faculty (8.7 percent of whom were faculty of color) reported the following:

- Academic rank distribution varies significantly across ethnic groups.
- The higher the rank, the lower the proportion of faculty of color is.
- Faculty of color are "less satisfied with nearly every aspect of their jobs" (1997, p. 25).

- Approximately 60 percent of the faculty of color report "somewhat extensive" to "extensive" stress regarding the review or promotion process (as compared to only 44 percent of White faculty).
- Faculty of color are more than twice as likely (49 percent) as White faculty (21 percent) to identify subtle discrimination as a source of stress.

Overall, minority faculty have more obstacles to their general satisfaction level than their White counterparts. Being a faculty member of color on campus often adds an element of unnecessary discomfort not experienced by majority faculty. As persons of distinct physical characteristics, faculty of color reported that their scholarly credentials can be largely ignored in campus scholarly settings while their skin color and other perceptible ethnic physical features and behaviors tend to be emphasized over their scholarly achievements (Turner and Myers, 1999). In other words, they felt that others responded to their outward racial or ethnic attributes rather than seeing them as colleagues and peers.

Another obstacle to faculty of color job satisfaction is the perception of tokenism. Some have reported being treated as token representatives, rather than as valued members of the faculty (Turner and Myers, 1999). They cited limited opportunities to develop working relationships with majority faculty (Elmore and Blackburn, 1983), and found little understanding, warmth, and empathy among their colleagues (Harvey and Scott-James, 1985). In fact, some faculty of color stated they felt so socially isolated by White colleagues that they were more comfortable interacting socially with their students of color (who may also feel quite isolated on the campus) (Turner and Myers, 1999). Because they frequently have a keen interest in racial or ethnic issues, faculty of color have been frequently typecast as ethnic specialists rather than as qualified experts in their disciplines (Garza, 1988).

As a culminating statement for this section of the chapter, we performed quantitative analyses of the National Study of Postsecondary Faculty 1993 (NSOPF 1993) consisting of the responses of more than twenty-five thousand faculty members nationwide (National Center for Education Statistics, 1993). We created reliable scales measuring global job satisfaction as well as satisfaction with students and teaching. We then performed a one-way analysis of variance to test for differences across racial groups. Although all three multivariate tests were significant ($p < .0001$), Tukey post hoc tests revealed very few pairwise differences. Comparing the different ethnic groups to Whites, we found that Whites report significantly more satisfaction with students than Asian Pacific Americans; and African Americans report higher satisfaction levels than Whites. With respect to satisfaction with teaching, the only significant pairwise comparison was that Whites report higher levels of satisfaction than Asian Pacific Americans. Finally, in the test of global job satisfaction, Whites were more satisfied than Asian Pacific Americans. However, it must be noted that the effect sizes of significant comparisons were quite small, indicating that overall and regardless of ethnicity, faculty report fairly similar levels of satisfaction. To be more specific, since satisfaction in all three categories was measured on a four-part scale (very dissatisfied to very satisfied), all averages hovered around three (somewhat satisfied).

How Do Faculty of Color Persevere and Survive with Respect to Tenure and Promotion?

Promotion and tenure reflect opportunities to advance through the faculty ranks and as such are considered the prime indicators of career success in academe. Limited opportunities for advancement through the ranks have been recorded for every minority racial or ethnic group except for Asian Pacific Americans (Brown, 1988; Astin, Antonio, Cress, and Astin, 1997; Turner and Myers, 1999). As a result, African Americans, American Indians, and Latinos are more likely to be concentrated at the lower levels of the professoriat (Nieves-Squires, 1991). A study by the National Urban League (1982) found that African American and Latino faculty cited lack of adequate publications as the major factor in denial of tenure. Clark (1989) indicated that the reward system based on research and publication for promoting faculty is more deeply rooted in academe "with every passing decade" (p. 5). The longer road to tenure may in part be due to the large blocks of time faculty of color report spending in advising and mentoring students of color, serving on multiple institutional committees (many of which have ties to diversity), or participating in community services (Cuádraz, 1998; Black, 1981; Blackwell, 1983; Nieves-Squires, 1991). It must be noted that all of the aforementioned activities are frequently undervalued when evaluating faculty for promotion and tenure (Garza, 1988; Washington and Harvey, 1989). Activities and responsibilities that seem to follow faculty of color leave little time to pursue the pure research needed at many universities for the granting of tenure.

According to an extensive study conducted in eight Midwestern states, Turner and Myers (1999) concluded that tenure and promotion may be especially problematic for faculty of color. Many reported being either told outright or indirectly that they did not fit "the profile" (p. 89) when they were not reappointed or denied tenure and promotion. Some faculty also stated that after not being reappointed or promoted, they were advised to relocate to other institutions, presumably to institutions of lower status with perceived lower standards where tenure and promotion for faculty from racial or ethnic groups might be more likely.

Again, we turned to the NSOPF 1993 for additional evidence. We looked at differences across racial groups on the reported proportion of time spent in various activities. We found that while Asian Pacific Americans report significantly more time spent in research than any other group, Whites reported spending significantly more time than other minorities.

However, African Americans report spending significantly more time in service than Whites. Finally, faculty of color reported spending significantly more time in informal contact with students outside of the classroom.

Do Faculty of Color Leave, Prematurely Forced Out by a Nonsupportive Atmosphere and Less-Than-Ideal Working Environment?

Faculty of color describe a working environment where subtle discrimination is experienced from

- Students who are unaccustomed or uncomfortable with people of color and thus respond in challenging or confrontational ways (de la Luz Reyes and Halcón, 1991; Jackson, 1991)
- Colleagues who either ignore them or make subtly racist comments about aspects such as appearance or linguistic skills (Padilla and Chávez, 1995; Turner and Myers, 1999)
- Overload due to new courses and excessive committee work (Garza, 1988; Cuádraz, 1998)
- Minimal guidance and mentoring toward reappointment, tenure, and promotion (Padilla and Chávez, 1995; Garza, 1988; Cuádraz, 1998; Turner and Myers, 1999)
- Disparagement of scholarly work due to a focus on racial or ethnic issues (de la Luz Reyes and Halcón, 1991; Tack and Patitu, 1992; Garza, 1988; Cuádraz, 1998)

Although not an exhaustive list, these points convey the type of hostile but mostly subtly racist work environment many faculty of color encounter daily in their institutions.

Faculty of color perceive they are expected to work harder than White faculty, or more directly put, work twice as hard to be treated as equal. Faculty of color sense they are "always in the spotlight" (Turner and Myers, 1999, p. 90), under constant scrutiny by their White colleagues. As such, they feel that they must consistently perform admirably and must constantly exceed White faculty in all situations.

However, do faculty of color leave their institutions at a greater rate than other faculty? While it may be true that some institutions have experienced what may be termed "the revolving door phenomenon," it must be emphasized that departure is not exclusively among faculty of color (Turner and Myers, 1999). Turner and Myers discovered that minorities hired in every rank outnumbered those who leave. Also, they noted that at the lower ranks, the ratio of Whites who leave to Whites hired is not much greater than the ratio of faculty of color who leave to the rate they are hired. At the higher ranks, the researchers found the number of White faculty who leave, due mainly to retirement, exceeds the number of Whites who are hired and also exceeds a comparable ratio among faculty of color. As such, Turner and Myers conclude that faculty of color underrepresentation cannot be blamed on turnover, but that it is more likely due to the problem of underhiring. They further suggest that *"demand-side* effects (such as strong affirmative action efforts) rather than *supply-side* effects (such as the absence—or perhaps perceived absence—of qualified candidates) have the greatest influence on minority hiring" (p. 135).

Despite the obstacles, Turner and Myers (1999) discovered that most faculty of color planned to remain in their chosen profession within the academy. To test Turner and Myer's assumption, we again turned to the NSOPF 1993. This time we looked at the proportion of faculty members who predicted that they were likely to leave their present faculty position for a different postsecondary institution. We found that whereas 20 percent of Whites predicted a change in institution, 31 percent of Latinos, 33 percent of American Indians, and 28 percent of African Americans reported a likely move. Therefore, although the majority of faculty of color may choose to remain in their chosen profession, a large number predict changing institutions.

What Specific Factors Contribute to Job Satisfaction Among Faculty of Color?

In this section of the chapter we relate areas that appear to increase the job satisfaction of faculty of color. These factors create numerous policy implications both for institutional researchers and others interested in studying the satisfaction of faculty on individual campuses.

Salary. Salaries have been typically used as a career barometer to measure status and equity in the workplace and have been shown to affect morale positively or negatively. Evidence strongly indicates that perceived inequities may cause more dissatisfaction than actual salary levels (Hagedorn, 1996) and thus may contribute to feelings of being undervalued. Therefore, if faculty of color perceive that their salary levels are somehow tied to their minority status or to their being an "only," dissatisfaction is more likely to occur.

Minority Affairs "Specialist." Another issue of discomfort is that all too often faculty of color find themselves placed in positions of being expected to handle minority affairs and speak as the minority expert. Moreover, as Turner and Myers (1999) point out, faculty members feel the pressure of being in a Catch-22 situation. On the one hand, they feel a responsibility to be a visible presence on campus in committees as the sole minority member and, on the other hand, they feel pressured to be change agents for issues that are of the utmost importance. Padilla (1994) identified activities such as these as a "cultural tax" that is payable in valuable time.

Turner and Myers (1999) concluded that faculty job satisfaction for faculty of color could be articulated into three themes: (1) satisfaction with teaching and working with students; (2) supportive administrative leadership, mentoring relationships, and collegiality; and (3) interaction with other faculty. A genuine love of teaching and interactions with students were identified as the most satisfying aspects of faculty of color's work lives.

Faculty of color assert that, when involved, administrative leaders (such as the provost, dean, or department chair) play an important role in encouraging and supporting them with resources and staff assistance. Many faculty also report the impact of mentor relationships on their professional lives, often citing at least several faculty and administrators they feel they could turn to for guidance. Some faculty of color also cite friendship and peer collaboration as significant in creating a more comfortable working environment. Finally, as one might expect, the very presence of other faculty of color in the workplace may lessen feelings of isolation, thus helping these individuals to become a more included part of the community.

In their national survey of the professoriat, Astin, Antonio, Cress, and Astin (1997) revealed areas of high levels of job satisfaction among faculty of color as compared to majority faculty, although the range among the groups still denotes some dissatisfaction. Most faculty of color cited intellectual challenge as the most important component of job satisfaction. Not unexpectedly, autonomy and independence in the workplace was another Slightly lower ratings for satisfaction in professional relations with other faculty surfaced in the findings. However, overall job satisfaction is lower and shows a wider range of differences than for White faculty.

Antonio's (1998) inquiry sheds a bit more light on the specific factors contributing to job satisfaction. In his sample, 82 percent of the faculty of color ranked developing a meaningful philosophy of life as a very important or essential personal goal as compared to 78 percent for White faculty. Also, 77 percent of the faculty of color ranked promoting racial understanding as a second important personal goal compared to only 58 percent for White faculty. A third important personal goal was helping others in difficulty, ranging from 83 percent for African American faculty to a low of 66 percent for White faculty.

Conclusions and Policies

For all faculty, the balancing of multiple duties of research, teaching, and service produces stress. McGrath (1976) posited that stress exists where the element of threat is related to the availability of resources for successfully meeting the demands of one's job. Sensitive administrators, especially the department chair and the program coordinator, can help mitigate stress with timely and committed assistance, especially during the pre-tenure time. Reducing the course load in the early pre-tenure years may give faculty of color time to develop new courses, attend to teaching and student needs, as well as provide time for research and writing. Providing support staff to attend to clerical tasks and graduate assistants to help with teaching and research can lighten the daily load considerably for all new faculty. Protecting faculty from accepting too many service commitments, such as committee assignments and dissertation committees, can also assist in freeing up more time to attend to scholarly work. In sum, what is of major importance in reducing stress is the extent to which departments and institutions in general are willing to commit their resources to aggressively address the problems that aggravate stress and job dissatisfaction and perpetuate the underrepresentation of faculty of color.

Mentoring newcomers to the organization and assisting them to become socialized to their new roles in the institution is common in the corporate world but much less so in academe. Yet the powerful force of mentoring and the success that results from mentoring relationships cannot be ignored in light of the positive outcomes they produce. As Padilla and Chávez (1995) remind us, many faculty of color who enter the academy did not have the benefit of mentors in graduate school, thus mentoring is much more critical for them, especially if the institution is serious about realizing the returns of its investment in these faculty.

Antonio (1998) notes that the value of faculty of color to higher education has not been subject to the same attention in research or debate. He points to "fairly indisputable reasons and imperatives" (p. 3) for examining the value of faculty of color, drawing from the literature (de la Luz Reyes and Halcón, 1991; Green, 1989; Mickelson and Oliver, 1991; Washington and Harvey, 1989) to illustrate five points. First, the proportional representation of faculty of color and the achievement of parity in academe speak directly to the American concept of equity in society. Second, faculty of color are essential for higher education in that they provide all students with diverse role models. Third, they assist in providing more effective mentoring for students of color. Fourth, they are supportive of minority-related and other areas of nontraditional scholarship and as such they bring new perspectives to academe. Fifth, in their sense of equity and democracy, faculty of color give students of color a greater voice in governance within their respective institutions.

The presence of faculty of color in the academy may be likened to the Greek god Janus with two faces. The first face depicts faculty of color as satisfied with many aspects of work and planning to remain in academe. The satisfied face smiles on the love of teaching, a sense of accomplishment, collegiality, interactions with other faculty of color, supportive administrators, and mentor relationships. Also seen as positive is the purposeful intent in doing research, choosing to focus on issues related to race and ethnicity. In addition, many faculty of color are committed to service to the larger community and are intent on making a difference in society.

Nonetheless, the second face of Janus indicates that all is not well in academe as illustrated so aptly by Cuádraz (1998) at the beginning of this chapter. To date, faculty of color are expected to enter the academy and adapt themselves to the majority culture and norms that dominate their institutional workplaces (Thompson and Dey, 1998). They enter academe marginalized into a larger academic community that does not provide them with full membership. As a new century dawns, we hope that faculty of color will not be expected to continue solely to adjust to the organizational environment as newcomers while the organization itself and the majority individuals within it remain static, unwilling to enact changes and organizational transformation in the academy.

In summary, faculty of color should not be forced to the borders of any institution because they are viewed as different. Rather, faculty of color must be recognized as valuable contributing members, and be welcomed as institutional transformers who are helping to move the academy from its static, traditional norms to new ways that fit students' and society's needs and realities in today's and tomorrow's world.

References

Antonio, A. L. "Faculty of Color Reconsidered: Retaining Scholars for the Future." Paper presented at Keeping Our Faculties: Addressing the Recruitment and Retention of Faculty of Color in Higher Education conference, Minneapolis, Minn., Oct. 1998.

Astin, H. S., Antonio, A. L., Cress, C. M., and Astin, A. W. *Race and Ethnicity in the American Professoriate, 1995–96.* Los Angeles: Higher Education Research Institute, University of California, 1997.

Black, A. S. "Affirmative Action and the Black Academic Situation." *Western Journal of Black Studies,* 1981, 5, 87–94.

Blackwell, J. "Strategies for Improving the Status of Blacks in Higher Education." *Planning and Changing,* 1983, 14, 56–73.

Brown, S. V. *Increasing Minority Faculty Recruitment: An Elusive Goal.* Princeton, N.J.: Educational Testing Service, 1988.

Clark, B. "The Absorbing Errand." *Educational Researcher,* 1989, 18, 1–14.

Cuádraz, G. H. "Questions Worth Asking: Observations from an Assistant Professor." Paper presented at Keeping Our Faculties: Addressing the Recruitment and Retention of Faculty of Color in Higher Education conference, Minneapolis, Minn., Oct. 1998.

de la Luz Reyes, M., and Halcón, J. J. "Practices of the Academy: Barriers to Access for Chicano Academics." In P. G. Altbach and K. Lomotey (eds.), *The Racial Crisis in American Higher Education.* Albany: State University of New York, 1991.

Elmore, C., and Blackburn, R. "Black and White Faculty in White Research Universities." *Journal of Higher Education,* 1983, 54, 1–15.

Gainen, J., and Boice, R. "Editors' Notes." In J. Gainen and R. Boice (eds.), *Building a Diverse Faculty.* New Directions for Teaching and Learning, no. 53. San Francisco: Jossey Bass, 1993.

Garza, H. "The 'Barrioization' of Hispanic Faculty." *Educational Record,* 1988, 69, 122–124.

Green, M. *Minorities on Campus: A Handbook for Enhancing Diversity.* Washington, D.C.: American Council on Education, 1989.

Hagedorn, L. S. "Wage Equity and Female Faculty Job Satisfaction: The Role of Wage Differentials in a Job Satisfaction Causal Model." *Research in Higher Education,* 1996, 37(5), 569–598.

Harvey, W., and Scott-James, D. "We Can't Find Any: The Elusiveness of Black Faculty in American Higher Education." *Issues in Education,* 1985, 3, 68–76.

Jackson, K. W. "Black Faculty in Academia." In P. G. Altbach and K. Lomotey (eds.), *The Racial Crisis in American Higher Education.* Albany: State University of New York, 1991.

Johnsrud, L. K., and Des Jarlais, C. D. "Barriers to Tenure for Women and Minorities." *Review of Higher Education,* 1994, 17, 335–353.

McGrath, J. E. "Stress and Behavioral Organizations." In M. Dunnette (ed.), *Handbook of Industrial and Organizational Psychology.* Chicago: Rand McNally, 1976.

Mickelson, M. L., and Oliver, M. L. "Making the Short List: Black Candidates and the Faculty Recruitment Process." In P. G. Altbach and K. Lomotey (eds.), *The Racial Crisis in American Higher Education.* Albany: State University of New York, 1991.

National Center for Education Statistics. *1993 National Study of Postsecondary Faculty.* Washington, D.C.: National Center for Education Statistics, 1993.

National Center for Education Statistics. *Digest of Educational Statistics 1998.* Washington, D.C.: U.S. Department of Education, 1999.

National Urban League. "Tri-State Minority Faculty Employment Opportunity Project, Final Report." New York: National Urban League, 1982. (ED 236 261)

Nieves-Squires, S. "Hispanic Women: Making Their Presence on Campus Less Tenuous." Washington, D.C.: Association of American Colleges, 1991. (ED 334 907)

Padilla, A. M. "Ethnic Minority Scholars, Research, and Mentoring: Current and Future Issues." *Educational Researcher,* 1994, *23,* 24–27.

Padilla, R. V., and Chávez, R. C. *The Leaning Ivory Tower: Latino Professors in American Universities.* Albany: State University of New York, 1995.

Smith, D. G., Wolf, L. E., and Busenberg, B. E. *Achieving Faculty Diversity: Debunking the Myths.* Washington, D.C.: Association of American Colleges and Universities, 1996.

Tack, M. W., and Patitu, C. L. *Faculty Job Satisfaction: Women and Minorities in Peril.* ASHE-ERIC Higher Education Report no. 5. Washington, D.C.: American Association for Higher Education, 1992.

Thompson, C. J., and Dey, E. L. "Pushed to the Margins: Sources of Stress for African American College and University Faculty." *Journal of Higher Education,* 1998, *69*(3), 324–345.

Turner, C.S.V., and Myers, S. L., Jr. *Faculty of Color in Academe: Bittersweet Success.* Needham Heights, Mass.: Allyn & Bacon, 1999.

Washington, V., and Harvey, W. *Affirmative Rhetoric, Negative Action: African-American and Hispanic Faculty at Predominantly White Institutions.* Report no. 2. Washington, D.C.: School of Education and Human Development, George Washington University, 1989.

BERTA VIGIL LADEN *is a postdoctoral fellow at Stanford University.*

LINDA SERRA HAGEDORN *is associate professor of higher education and chair of the Community College Leadership program at the University of Southern California.*

6

This chapter focuses on the role of the sabbatical leave in the development, satisfaction, and productivity of faculty in postsecondary institutions. An examination of the origin, definition, purposes, and outcomes of sabbatical leaves reviewed in the literature clarifies the role and benefits of the sabbatical leave.

The Role and Benefits of the Sabbatical Leave in Faculty Development and Satisfaction

Celina M. Sima

The very first sabbatical leave was offered at Harvard University by President Charles Elliot in 1880 (Eells and Hollins, 1962). Elliot made this first sabbatical offer of every seventh year off in an attempt to lure a scholar away from Johns Hopkins University. Since that time, sabbatical leaves have continued as a cherished part of academic life. Since the mid-1990s, the discussion of faculty productivity has become commonplace and a considerable portion of the debate has been focused on sabbatical policy. College and university trustees, state legislators, and the public have questioned the role and benefit of the sabbatical leave. Within the context of this tension between academic culture and public concern for accountability, this chapter reviews the relationship between the roles and benefits of sabbatical leave and the development and satisfaction of the members of college and university faculty.

Understanding the Tension

The controversy surrounding sabbatical leaves begins with the historical roots of the term *sabbatical*. Bruce A. Kimball (1978) has traced the origin of the sabbatical to the ancient Hebrew Sabbath and the sabbatical year. In an article entitled "The Origin of the Sabbath and Its Legacy to the Modern Sabbatical," Kimball explains in some detail the connection between the biblical reference to the day of rest and the practice of sabbatical leave within academe.

Many articles and books on the topic of sabbatical leaves include a discussion of the connection between the biblical reference and current sabbatical policy and practice (Kimball, 1978; Tiedje and Collins, 1996; Zahorski, 1994). These references to the day of rest or the year to allow the fields to lie fallow shed some light on the popular belief that the sabbatical leave provides only the opportunity for faculty to rest and relax. This type of popular public perception was manifested in a 1994 sabbatical decision in Colorado that ultimately led to a serious threat to sabbatical leaves in the entire state. Kit Lively (1994) reported that a powerful legislator introduced a bill to regulate faculty sabbaticals and abolish administrative leaves. This action arose from news that a leave was granted to a highly paid administrator who was stepping down from his position. He used the leave time to retool by reading Aristotle and Shakespeare in order to reactivate his sense of scholarship. James E. Sultan Jr., the senior academic officer for the Colorado Commission on Higher Education, stated that while this sabbatical request would not be interpreted as a vacation to those in academe, it read like that to the general public. Lively reported that the public reaction to this report was swift and indignant. Consequently, the chancellor of the Colorado Springs campus withdrew his approval of the sabbatical leave. That 1994 incident ultimately tightened the sabbatical leave policy and procedures in Colorado and sparked further discussion and review across the country.

Not only the public and their legislative representatives but also the college or university granting the sabbatical leave expect the sabbatical to be a productive endeavor. Thus, faculty members shoulder the burden of proving that their sabbatical leave will bring benefits to the college, their discipline, or the population in general. A 1962 (Eells and Hollins) examination of sabbatical policy revealed that within academe this type of leave carries an expectation that the time away from the campus will yield significant benefits to the campus in research productivity, improved teaching, or to a lesser degree, increased service to the campus. These findings are supported by a number of researchers who have reported on sabbatical policy and practice since that early study was conducted (Boening and Miller, 1997; Sima and Denton, 1995; Tiedje and Collins, 1996; Zahorski, 1994). It is clear that the goals of the public, academic institutions, and faculty members are far more similar than the controversy would imply. It is equally obvious that those in academe must inform the public about the definitions, purposes, and the expected and actual outcomes of the faculty sabbatical leave.

The Definition and Purpose of the Sabbatical Leave

In *The Sabbatical Mentor,* Zahorski (1994) provides both a traditional definition of the sabbatical leave as well as suggestions for additional characteristics to make it more contemporary. He begins with Carter Good's (1959) definition: "[The sabbatical leave is] a plan for providing teachers with an opportunity for self-improvement through a leave of absence with full or partial compensation following a designated number of years of consecutive service (originally after six years)" (p. 424). Zahorski adds that faculty must be required to return to service after the leave and must file a sabbatical report. Although specific university policies may differ, the definitions found in literature of the last decade generally conform to the hybrid definition set forth by Good and Zahorski. Together, Good and Zahorski provide a definition that conveys the serious nature of the sabbatical leave. During the leave, some sort of faculty development is expected. Such compensation is only granted after a number of years of service to the institution. A report of activities must be filed after the sabbatical leave is complete to address productivity concerns. Further, the faculty member is expected to return to service after completing the sabbatical leave.

Despite the high degree of agreement on the definition of sabbatical leaves, there is less agreement regarding its purposes. Zahorski identified four purposes drawn from institutional policy statements: to provide opportunity for scholarly enrichment, to improve teaching, to promote course and curriculum development, and to enhance artistic performance and creative growth. Overall he stated that the "function of sabbatical leave is to stimulate a faculty member's professional, personal, and creative growth" (1994, p. 8).

A recent study (Sima and Denton, 1995) reported eight purposes for which sabbatical leave might be granted: to conduct research, to engage in uninterrupted study, to write journal articles or a book, to enhance artistic performance and creative growth, to improve teaching, to promote course and curriculum development, for refreshment, to provide new experiences and travel, and to complete graduate work (Bowen and Schuster, 1986; Daugherty, 1979; Ingraham and Kingt, 1965; Rudolph,1990; Zahorski, 1994).

A pilot test using this list of sabbatical purposes conducted with responses from faculty who had written their sabbatical plans revealed even further specificity in their purpose statements. Their primary anticipated activities included the following: to learn a new technique, to develop their research, to conduct research, to study, to write, to conduct reviews or create art work, and to develop courses or curricula.

In a study of the sabbatical leave among nursing faculty, Tiedje and Collins (1996) connected the discussion of the purpose and the process of sabbatical indicating that the obsolescence of people and ideas is a constant threat. They viewed the sabbatical leave as an opportunity for faculty to study at other institutions or to focus on self-study closer to home. They also reported on the sabbatical as providing a chance to learn something new, whether in a scientific laboratory or a more practitioner-oriented survey research center. Finally, they suggested that the opportunity for new collaborative grant-writing efforts or less tangible consultations with others in related fields might lead to new perspectives or ideas.

Sarason (1990) focused on another purpose of the sabbatical leave: a shift in the balance of faculty responsibilities. He reported that the purpose of the sabbatical is to "free the person from all teaching and administrative responsibilities and to encourage him or her to review past accomplishments, or to take stock, or to move in new directions, or to go somewhere to learn something new. . . . The sabbatical is not a gift from the university. It is recognition that there has to be a time when you can take distance from your accustomed routine so that when you return there will be an infusion of new energy and new ideas" (p. 138).

While the purposes for sabbatical leaves may differ from one campus to another and from one individual faculty member to another, it appears that university administrators and faculty members agree that the leave period should have a clear purpose and should result in outcomes that are of long-range benefit to the university. Moreover, the sabbatical leave should be productive and important from the faculty member's own viewpoint.

Who Is Eligible, and How Many Faculty Take Sabbatical Leaves?

Eligibility for a sabbatical leave differs from one institution to another, but generally a faculty member is eligible after six years of uninterrupted service to the university. Sabbatical leaves are most often granted after the faculty member has attained tenure. Zahorski (1994) points out an emerging trend of sabbatical leaves being granted to junior faculty after only two to three years of service. This policy may prove to support the successful attainment of tenure, particularly in institutions where the attainment of strong records specifically of research is highly desirable.

In a recent edition of *The Chronicle of Higher Education*, Robin Wilson (1999) reported that while "the number of professors on sabbatical in a given year varies from campus to campus, at public universities the proportion typically hovers around 5 percent," while it is much larger at private elite institutions. Wilson illustrated this point by using Swarthmore College as an example. At Swarthmore, as many as 20 percent of the 160 full-time faculty members may be on sabbatical leaves each year. Wilson's findings are also consistent with the Sima and Denton (1995) study of a public research university which found that on average, over a given three-year period, 3.8 percent of the faculty go on sabbatical leaves each year. Approximately half of the faculty in the study indicated that some proportion of their sabbatical would involve travel outside of the state or outside of the country.

Why Is the Sabbatical Leave Particularly Important in the Academic Setting?

What unique characteristics of academe make a sabbatical leave an important element of college and university life? While no empirical data is available regarding the relative importance of sabbatical leaves in academe versus other settings, there is much anecdotal discussion. The typical faculty member begins to prepare for research, teaching, and service responsibilities during graduate school. The subject matter that is studied in the graduate program provides the base for research and teaching assistantships. The newly minted Ph.D. enters the job market with a cutting-edge understanding of the literature and the scholarly discourse surrounding that literature. That information provides the foundation for course development and for research projects and grants. As the years pass, faculty must work hard to keep up with the emerging literature as they carry out the duties and responsibilities of their positions. This leaves little time to respond to significant shifts in the discipline, their program of research, or the curriculum. In part because of the success of academe in pushing forward on research frontiers, research programs can shift dramatically. Promising findings, while highly desirable, can result in a particular line of research drying up. Grant support is not likely to be forthcoming in areas of research where the perception may be that most of the important questions have been addressed. In such cases as these, the sabbatical leave may play a critical role. It may provide a valuable space in the academic career to explore new lines of research; to respond to shifting research agendas through fresh familiarity with a new literature or the development of new research techniques; to write grant proposals; or to publish recent research findings (Ciampa, 1978; Sima and Denton, 1995; Tiedje and Collins, 1996; Zahorski, 1994).

Although faculty are freed of teaching and service responsibilities during the leave, sabbatical leaves may also be used to focus on these aspects of faculty life. The intensity of the regular teaching schedule leaves little time for substantive changes in present course offerings, the development of new courses, or the development of new programs. The sabbatical leave provides the significant time commitment needed to update a course to introduce technology enhancements, to develop a new course that introduces students to emerging theories or methods, or to develop a new program that may be more responsive to professional communities (Kang and Miller, 1998; Sima and Denton, 1995; Zahorski, 1994).

The service component of academic life also requires periodic renewal. Campus-level service responsibilities such as committee work or campus governance are not an emphasis during the sabbatical leave. However, there are other forms of service—to the discipline, to the profession, or to other university stakeholders—that arise as a focus of the sabbatical leave. Leave time can allow for the development of an editorship, professional organization leadership, the establishment of a center or institute, or leadership in a community-based planning effort. These types of service activities are often of as much benefit to the academic institution as they are to the individual faculty member.

The periodic opportunity to retool and redirect efforts may well benefit each role that a faculty member performs. This demand for continuous cutting-edge knowledge acquisition, development, and dissemination is not typical of the vast majority of careers. However, it is interesting to note that the sabbatical leave is used in other professions where multiple and similar demands exist. Increasingly, the business world is using the sabbatical leave rather than letting go of midcareer researchers or managers who merely require a period for retooling (Toomey and Connor, 1988).

Benefits of a Sabbatical Leave

The present section substantiates the importance of the sabbatical leave in academe by reviewing the evidence of benefits of the sabbatical. Zahorski's (1994) review of six benefits of the sabbatical for faculty provides the framework for this discussion.

The first benefit of the sabbatical is that it serves as an agent of rejuvenation and renewal. According to Zahorski, faculty members report that the opportunity to break away from the usual routine "has enormous restorative potential, renewing faculty not only physically, but mentally and spiritually as well" (p. 116). The direct reference to renewal and regeneration as a positive outcome was made in two other reports. Jarecky and Sandifer (1986) referred to the spirit of renewal that was apparent in the generally enthusiastic descriptions written by the medical school faculty who had taken sabbaticals. Avakian (1986–87) reported that even in a sabbatical report in which faculty members reported not being as productive as anticipated, the sabbatical activities appeared to be "just as uplifting, recreative, and regenerative as those cited in the reports of other leave recipients" (p. 28).

The second benefit is that a sabbatical leave provides a time for reflection. Without the usual time constraints, faculty members have an opportunity to reflect on their careers and the direction of their work. This reflection may help faculty to redirect their teaching, research, and service goals.

Third, a sabbatical leave furnishes a fresh perspective. Zahorski (1994) identified a few ways in which this perspective is manifested. Increased time for reflection helps in creating a fresh view of ideas and movements in the field. Time away from campus can also increase appreciation for the academic community and the colleagues within that community. Travel raises awareness of different customs or traditions that may be highly desirable to incorporate into one's routine in the future. Zahorski also reported that some faculty members realize some of the limits of their productivity and get more in tune with their own strengths and weaknesses.

Fourth, the sabbatical leave provides an opportunity to build new professional relationships. Faculty have reported that their visits with colleagues at other institutions often resulted in long-term collegial relationships. Thus, time away from a faculty member's home institution may broaden opportunities for collaboration in future research, service, or teaching projects.

Fifth, a sabbatical leave provides opportunities to become or to stay current in the discipline. Zahorski reminds readers that in some fields it is very difficult to maintain cutting-edge knowledge. In fact, in some areas, specifically those that are more technologically oriented, it may not even be possible to remain current by relying solely on the reading of the latest journals and texts. A sabbatical leave provides the flexibility and time to visit labs or field sites where the most recent information is in the making. Sorcinelli (1986) also notes the importance of learning new things and taking on new challenges; these activities help faculty "to enhance unique strengths and interests, or to rethink what to do in a career" (p. 15).

Sixth, Zahorski (1994) asserts that the sabbatical enhances teaching. The focus on improved scholarship brings relevance to the classroom; the infusion of new findings into classroom curricula brings new energy and confidence. Zahorski also reminds us that many faculty members take classes during their sabbatical leave. This experience exposes faculty to the pedagogy of peers and gives faculty a heightened awareness of the perspective of students. While Boice (1987) warns that released time from teaching responsibility may convey a negative message about teaching, most researchers have found that an important benefit of a sabbatical leave is the enhancement of teaching (Boening and Miller, 1997; Kang and Miller, 1998; Russell, 1984; Sima and Denton, 1995; Zahorski, 1994).

As for benefits to the institution, Zahorski identifies eight: increased faculty efficiency, versatility, and productivity; strengthened institutional programs; enhanced learning environment, improved morale; enhanced loyalty to the institution; enhanced faculty recruitment and retention; enhanced intellectual climate; and enhanced academic reputation. While he has identified a list of benefits to individuals and to the institution, it is clear that the benefits can reach from the individual to the institution and to society at large.

In a study by Sima and Denton (1995), a rather impressive list of tangible products of sabbatical were found through an examination of the postsabbatical reports of 125 faculty members. For the three-year period examined, faculty produced forty-two books or manuscripts, twenty-six book chapters, and four monographs; published ninety-one articles; submitted sixty-five papers for publication; secured $1,315,000 in research grants; submitted thirty-six grant proposals; gave ninety-four talks, presentations, or invited lectures; developed thirteen new or revised courses; and prepared two music compositions, one conference, and one analytical report. It appears that the beneficiaries of this work extended beyond the faculty.

Faculty Development and Satisfaction

Clearly, the literature points to the sabbatical as a unique and important factor in faculty development and satisfaction. In fact, in only one study was a sabbatical leave found to be of no benefit in improving faculty scholarly productivity (Boice, 1987).

As for satisfaction in particular, the literature reveals faculty have very positive reports regarding their experiences during and after the sabbatical leave. Only one study actually focused on faculty satisfaction. Jarecky and Sandifer (1986) interviewed seventy medical school faculty members at seven institutions. They reported that 80 percent of the participants viewed the sabbatical experience as very favorable; the authors judged that three out of every four had accomplished something substantial such as writing research papers or books or reorganizing teaching programs. The authors further reported that a spirit of renewal was apparent in the generally enthusiastic descriptions provided by those who had taken a sabbatical leave. Many emphasized increased self-confidence in their professional abilities.

Conclusion

To date, the research regarding the sabbatical leave reveals that in general faculty members benefit from and are satisfied with their sabbatical leave experiences. These studies provide some insight about the ways in which the sabbatical leave facilitates faculty development and productivity. The findings also reveal the benefits of sabbatical leave that accrue to the home institution—increased productivity, improved programs, strengthened intellectual climate, and enhanced academic reputation.

In the future, research should continue to examine the role and benefits of sabbatical leaves. However, in order to ensure that sabbatical policies continue to be offered by postsecondary institutions, the academic community must now examine and report the relationship between the sabbatical leave and the benefits that accrue to the community and society. In addition, academe must find effective means of communicating these benefits to legislators and other stakeholders who may influence the sabbatical policies of the future.

References

Avakian, A. N. "Planning for Innovative Leave Opportunities." *Planning for Higher Education,* 1986–1987, *15,* 23–28.

Boening, C., and Miller, M. "Research and Literature on the Sabbatical Leave: A Review." 1997. Available from the ERIC Document Reproduction Service, (800) 443-ERIC. (ED 414 777)

Boice, Robert. "Is Released Time an Effective Component of Faculty Development Programs?" *Research in Higher Education,* 1987, *26,* 311–326.

Bowen, H., and Schuster, J. *American Professors: A National Resource Imperiled.* New York: Oxford University Press, 1986.

Ciampa, B. J. "Faculty Development: The 'Haves' and 'Have-Nots.'" *Research in Education,* Feb. 1978, pp. 1–18.

Daugherty, H., Jr. "Sabbatical Leaves in Higher Education." Unpublished doctoral dissertation, Indiana University, Bloomington, 1979.

Eells, W., and Hollins, E. "Sabbatical Leave in American Higher Education." *U.S. Office of Education Bulletin.* Bulletin no. 17. 1962.

Good, C. (ed.). *Dictionary of Education.* (3rd ed.) New York: McGraw-Hill, 1959.

Ingraham, M., and King, F. *The Outer Fringe: Faculty Benefits Other Than Annuities and Insurance.* Madison: University of Wisconsin, 1965.

Jarecky, R. K., and Sandifer, M. G. "Faculty Members' Evaluations of Sabbaticals." *Journal of Medical Education,* 1986, *61,* 803–807.

Kang, B., and Miller, M. T. "Sabbatical as a Form of Faculty Renewal in the Community College: Green Pastures or Fallow Fields?" Research report, 1998. Available from the ERIC Document Reproduction Service, (800) 443-ERIC. (ED 417 778)

Kimball, B. A. "The Origin of the Sabbath and Its Legacy to the Modern Sabbatical." *Journal of Higher Education,* 1978, *49,* 303–315.

Lively, K. "Sabbaticals Under Fire." *Chronicle of Higher Education,* Feb. 23, 1994, p. A16.

Rudolph, F. *The American College and University.* Athens: University of Georgia, 1990.

Russell, T. "The Teaching Connection." *Academic Therapy,* 1984, *19*(4), 437–441.

Sarason, S. B. *The Predictable Failure of School Reform.* San Francisco: Jossey-Bass, 1990.

Sima, C. M., and Denton, W. E. "Reasons for and Products of Faculty Sabbatical Leaves." Paper presented at the annual meeting of the Association for the Study of Higher Education, Orlando, Fla., Nov. 1995.

Sorcinelli, M. D. "Sabbaticals and Leaves: Critical Events in the Careers of Faculty." Paper presented at the annual meeting of the American Educational Research Association, San Francisco, Apr. 1986.

Tiedje, L. B., and Collins C. "The Sabbatical Year: Letting the Fields Lay Fallow." *Nursing Outlook,* 1996, *44,* 235–238.

Toomey, E. L., and Connor, J. M. "Employee Sabbaticals: Who Benefits and Why." *Personnel,* 1988, *65,* 81–84.

Wilson, R. "The Stay-at-Home Sabbatical Increases in Popularity." *Chronicle of Higher Education,* July 23, 1999, p. A16.

Zahorski, K. J. *The Sabbatical Mentor: A Practical Guide to Successful Sabbaticals.* Bolton, Mass.: Anker, 1994.

CELINA M. SIMA is associate dean for academic affairs and courtesy associate professor at the University of Illinois at Chicago.

7

The number of full- and part-time faculty members ineligible for tenure has increased rapidly in the past decade. Their employment conditions and levels of satisfaction are the focus of this chapter.

The New Faculty Majority: Somewhat Satisfied but Not Eligible for Tenure

Judith M. Gappa

The majority of faculty teaching in American colleges and universities today are not eligible for tenure; their appointments either explicitly state that tenure is not an option or they teach in institutions that do not grant tenure. This new faculty majority may be employed either part- or full-time. According to the 1993 National Study of Postsecondary Faculty (NSOPF 1993), 42 percent of all faculty are employed part-time; 96 percent of them are ineligible for tenure (Gappa and Leslie, 1997, pp. 9, 12). In addition, 28 percent of all full-time faculty occupy positions which do not lead to tenure (Leatherman, 1999). Perhaps of even greater importance is the rate at which the number of faculty not eligible for tenure has increased. For example, the percentage of part-timers jumped from approximately 35 percent in 1987 to 42 percent in 1993 (Gappa and Leslie, 1993; Leslie, 1998a). During the same period, full-time faculty not eligible for tenure climbed from 19 to 28 percent of the total workforce; those on tenure track fell from 29 percent to 20 percent (Leatherman, 1999, p. 14).

Faculty members ineligible for tenure are found in significant numbers in all types of institutions and in most disciplines. Although part-timers are hired primarily to teach on short-term appointments (Gappa and Leslie, 1993, 1997), full-time faculty ineligible for tenure have more varied roles, types of appointments, and responsibilities as teachers, researchers, and clinicians (Gappa, 1996, National Education Association, 1996).

A paramount concern of higher education institutions with their increasing enrollments and declining resources is ensuring that members of the new faculty majority are consistently high quality performers in the classroom as well as in their other assignments. High quality performers are usually satisfied employees. This chapter explores the levels of satisfaction of faculty ineligible for tenure by looking first at the employment conditions and reasons underlying variations in the satisfaction of part-timers and then at the differing types of appointments and levels of satisfaction among full-timers. The chapter concludes with recommendations aimed at increasing the satisfaction of tenure-ineligible faculty through fair employment practices and inclusion as valued members of the faculty.

Part-Time Faculty

Hired primarily to teach, part-time faculty members are represented in substantial numbers in all types of institutions. They are especially well represented in community colleges, where over 60 percent of faculty are part-timers. Thirty-nine percent of the faculty at comprehensive colleges and universities and 36 percent at private liberal arts colleges are part-timers. Research and doctoral universities use proportionately fewer part-timers (23 and 32 percent respectively), because they also rely on graduate teaching assistants. Similarly, individual disciplines also use part-timers in different proportions. Fields in which part-timers are 49 percent or more of the faculty are: law (61 percent), fine arts (51 percent), English and literature (50 percent), computer science (49.5 percent), and mathematics and statistics (49 percent). They are also well represented in engineering (32 percent), education (45 percent), business (47 percent), health sciences (36 percent), humanities (45 percent), and natural and social sciences (37 percent). The lowest levels of part-time faculty are in agriculture and home economics (20 percent), economics (23 percent), political science (25 percent), and the biological and physical sciences (26 and 27 percent respectively) (Leslie, 1998a) The reliance on part-time faculty in fields such as business, health, and law is in keeping with their value as practitioners in professional fields. The reliance on part-time faculty in English and mathematics is different. In these disciplines they are employed in large numbers to replace full-time teachers in core academic subjects (Benjamin, 1998). Both Leslie and Benjamin recommend further study of part-timers' characteristics and levels of satisfaction discipline by discipline.

Who They Are, What They Do. Most part-timers (77 percent) have other jobs outside academe. For 64 percent, the part-time academic responsibility is added to their full-time employment. Mean household income for part-timers is $67,637 compared to $81,248 for full-time faculty. Individual part-time faculty members are the principal income producers in their households, averaging $48,743, of which their pay for teaching averages $10,180 per year (Leslie, 1998b). Despite their part-time affiliation with their college or university, part-timers appear to be committed to their employing institutions. On average part-timers have occupied their present teaching position for 6.3 years versus 11.2 years for full-timers (Leslie, 1998b). Although only 15 percent of part-timers hold the doctoral degree with an additional 11 percent holding a professional degree, most (52 percent) have one or more master's degrees (Leslie, 1998a; Gappa and Leslie, 1997). The most striking difference between part- and full-time faculty is gender: women are much more likely to be employed as part-timers than as full-timers (45 percent compared with 33 percent) (Leslie, 1998b). For the most part, part-time faculty members appear to be reasonably well-off in economic terms and professionally qualified for the work they do. The differences among part-timers and full-timers are not as great as they are assumed to be. One could conclude that they constitute a community of professional peers (Gappa and Leslie, 1997).

Part-timers teach for a variety of reasons. In *The Invisible Faculty* (1993), Gappa and Leslie described them as belonging to one of four general categories. The majority of part-timers are employed elsewhere in their primary careers as "professionals, specialists, or experts" (p. 50). These part-timers are motivated to teach because of their intrinsic satisfaction with the work itself and their dedication to teaching and to the constituencies they serve. Most have an altruistic desire to help others, particularly those who come from similar backgrounds. Other part-timers, "the career enders" (p. 49), are in life transitions to retirement or are retired. Some part-timers, "the freelancers" (p. 60), prefer working simultaneously in a variety of positions, one of which is part-time teaching.

Part-timers aspiring to full-time, tenure-track faculty positions, labeled as "aspiring academics" (p. 54), represent only 16 percent of the total. However, over 36 percent of the part-timers in the humanities versus 1.5 percent in the health sciences seek tenure-track positions. Sixty-five percent of part-timers in the fine arts and 61 percent of those in the humanities reported they were teaching part-time because full-time jobs were not available in academe or elsewhere (Leslie, personal correspondence, Sept. 28, 1999; Leslie 1998a). These aspiring academics generally teach for economic reasons, sometimes at several campuses simultaneously, hoping that eventually they will achieve a tenure-track position (Gappa and Leslie, 1993).

Colleges and universities seek part-time faculty for many reasons. The expansion of community colleges and the leveling off of state support for higher education in the early 1990s are the most compelling. From 1970 to 1995 the number of faculty members at two-year institutions grew by 210 percent compared with 69 percent growth in four-year institutions. The proportion of part-time faculty not eligible for tenure in community colleges has risen from 50 percent to 60 percent (Leslie, 1998b; Wyles, 1998). Increasing enrollment, financial hard times, and the need for flexibility have made institutions more wary about long-term commitments to tenure, especially when a talented workforce who will accept employment with lower salaries, shorter time commitments, and no benefits is readily available. In addition, the loss of control over mandatory retirement, the preference of some individuals for part-time work, and the lack of evidence that part-timers teach any less effectively have contributed to the use of part-timers (Leslie, 1998b; Haeger, 1998).

Thus, both colleges and universities and part-timers benefit from part-time employment. Eighty-five percent of part-time faculty report they are somewhat or very satisfied with their jobs (Gappa and Leslie, 1997). However, while they express satisfaction with their teaching assignments, they are dissatisfied with various aspects of their employment.

Employment Policies. Part-timers are heterogeneous, with highly varied life circumstances and motivations for teaching, but their employment conditions are not. Regardless of the quality of their performance, length of their employment, qualifications for their positions, or the needs of the institution, part-timers in most colleges and universities are employed under what many may label as exploitative practices.

Part-time faculty employment tends to be a casual affair based on informal practices and commitments within departments rather than on centrally promulgated and monitored institutional policies that provide fair and consistent treatment. In good circumstances, part-timers become valued and established colleagues despite the informality and insecurity of their employment. In the worst circumstances, part-timers remain marginal and are subject to capricious and arbitrary treatment (Gappa and Leslie, 1993, 1997).

Recruitment. In contrast to the rigorous national recruitment of tenure-track faculty, recruitment of part-timers is usually informal and handled by department chairs. Some vacancies are advertised regionally or locally, but most recruiting is by word of mouth. Bottom-fishing for the least expensive and most vulnerable (but not necessarily best qualified) can occur when department chairs are not accountable for their hiring practices.

Appointments. Most part-timers are appointed term by term and notification of an appointment or renewal (regardless of the numbers of semesters previously employed) often comes very late. Thus, part-timers are left with little time to prepare, which can have a deleterious effect on the quality of their teaching performance. For those part-timers dependent upon the income, failure to be notified in a timely fashion can seriously disrupt their lives.

Term-by-term appointments, policies limiting the numbers of continuous appointments possible, and arbitrary limits on the amount of work part-timers can be assigned contribute to the insecurity that part-timers feel about their employment and may keep them from qualifying for benefits. These are unfortunate consequences of the institution's desire to retain flexibility or its unnecessary worries that continuous employment without interruption could lead to de facto tenure.

Support, Services, and Benefits. Resources for support services, supplies, equipment, and office space are scarce and part-timers usually receive the lowest priority. Frequently, offices that supply services require part-timers to turn in requests far in advance and are closed during evenings and weekends, when many part-timers teach. Unavailability of adequate support services or office space can hamper part-timers' teaching and make meeting with their students difficult if not impossible.

Salaries. Salary policies for part-timers vary greatly depending on institutional culture and ability to pay. Part-timers' views about their salaries also vary. Those employed full-time elsewhere are generally less concerned; others dependent on their salaries as an important source of income want a fair wage and merit increases. The vast majority of institutions use either a flat rate for all part-timers or an established range, frequently defined on the basis of qualifications or seniority. However, some institutions are inconsistent in their salary policies. In rare circumstances part-timers are able to negotiate their salaries with high-level administrators individually, thus leading to complete erosion of salary policies.

Benefits. Very few institutions provide benefits for part-timers. The three benefits most important to part-timers are: subsidized medical insurance (available to 17 percent of part-timers and 97 percent of full-timers), subsidized retirement plans (available to 20 percent of part-timers and 93 percent of full timers), and tuition grants or waivers (available to 9 percent of part-timers and 48 percent of full-timers) (Gappa and Leslie, 1993). Because institutions formulate benefits policies according to the time base of an individual's appointment rather than years of service, part-time faculty with ten to fifteen years of continuous teaching experience are usually treated the same as part-timers hired to teach for one semester. Lack of benefits was the issue receiving the highest response of dissatisfaction (90 percent) on the NSOPF 1993 (Gappa and Leslie, 1997).

Job Security. Many part-timers have enjoyed long and mutually productive associations with their colleges and universities, but these stable employment histories resulted from institutional goodwill, not from any right part-timers have to job security. Part-timers believe that a system in which long service and distinguished performance do not ensure continuing employment is unfair.

Status in the Academic Community. For the most part, part-timers express anger and frustration about their second-class status and the lack of appreciation for their efforts. Instead of feeling connected to or integrated into campus life, they often feel alienated, powerless, and invisible. This is frequently due to departmental culture and the leadership (or lack thereof) of department chairs. Many part-timers expressed annoyance about the lack of consultation and involvement in campus or departmental decisions affecting them, an annoyance that is exacerbated by the knowledge that protesting could jeopardize their continued employment (Gappa and Leslie, 1993).

Effect of Employment Conditions on Satisfaction. In summary, part-timers responding to the NSOPF 1993 said they experienced intrinsic satisfaction from teaching, but were dissatisfied with many aspects of their employment. While 85 percent of part-timers and full-timers expressed overall satisfaction with their jobs, their satisfaction with various aspects of their jobs varied considerably. In contrast to full-time faculty, 45 percent of part-timers expressed dissatisfaction with job security. Part-time and full-time faculty also differed substantially in their level of satisfaction with opportunities for advancement: fifty-six percent of part-timers were very or somewhat dissatisfied, while 64 percent of full-timers were very or somewhat satisfied. Both groups of faculty clustered in the middle range of moderate satisfaction or dissatisfaction with salary. However, the differences are most telling with regard to benefits: 75 percent of full-timers expressed satisfaction while 90 percent of part-timers said they were somewhat or very dissatisfied (Gappa and Leslie, 1997).

Using the NSOPF 1993, Benjamin (1998) studied the satisfaction and dissatisfaction of part-timers in four-year institutions according to whether they taught in a vocationally oriented or liberal arts discipline. His analysis indicated that the vocationally oriented part-timers were substantially higher than the liberal arts part-timers in their overall satisfaction, as well as in their satisfaction with benefits, salary, job security, and time to keep current in the field. He found that the liberal arts faculty members had substantial reasons for their greater discontent. They were more dependent on their part-time employment even though their household income was lower on average, since job security and health and other benefits did not come as frequently from another employer. Benjamin concluded that the liberal arts faculty's feelings of being economically vulnerable and constrained are cause for concern as faculty teach a substantial part of the lower-division undergraduate curriculum.

Ultimately, the satisfaction levels of part-timers with their academic employment can have a direct bearing on the quality of their teaching. Leslie, Benjamin, and others have recommended more research into the differences in the use of part-timers among disciplines and types of institutions and the relationships of those differences to satisfaction levels.

Full-Time Faculty Ineligible for Tenure

In response to the excessive use of part-timers by some institutions, colleges and universities with tenure systems are employing more full-time faculty ineligible for tenure. For example, Georgia State University's College of Arts and Sciences reduced the number of courses taught by part-timers from nine hundred to 227 and added sixty-five new full-time faculty members this year. Part-timers typically earned $2,000 a course or up to $16,000 a year for a full load. The new full-time instructors will earn $24,000 to $30,000 and receive benefits (Wilson, 1999).

Full-time, tenure-ineligible faculty are employed to: achieve more continuity in academic programs; staff entire areas of the curriculum; focus on one particular area of faculty responsibility such as teaching, research or clinical practice; or add significant experience and expertise available only outside academe (Gappa, 1996). According to the NSOPF 1993, the heaviest concentration of such faculty was in the research universities (39.5 percent), followed by doctorate-granting (18.5 percent), comprehensive (16.9 percent), community colleges (12.3 percent), and private liberal arts colleges (7.8 percent). The health sciences employed the largest percentage of such faculty (28 percent), followed by the natural sciences (15.7 percent) and the humanities (12.5 percent). While 83 percent of these faculty were hired in teaching appointments, either full-time or in conjunction with other duties (National Education Association, 1996), they were also employed as research professors, professors of practice, and distinguished senior lecturers. For example, the medical schools have used full-time nontenurable faculty appointments for years, primarily in clinical positions (Gappa, 1996). By 1981, 72 percent of the 112 U.S. medical schools had nontenurable tracks. From 1983–1993, the total number of clinical faculty in medical schools nearly doubled while the percentage in tenure-track or tenured positions declined (Jones and Sanderson, 1994).

When institutions consolidate part-time faculty positions into full-time appointments for the purposes of teaching undergraduates or specialized areas of the curriculum, the full-timers generally are treated better than the part-timers they replace. These appointments typically are for one year or longer, either renewable without limit or of fixed duration with limited renewals. Compensation is better than that of part-timers and includes benefits. Most receive funding for professional development. However, these faculty members frequently experience some status differentials, such as rights to participation in governance or to receive sabbatical leaves. For some teaching faculty, job security is a critical issue, depending on the nature of their contract (Gappa, 1996; National Education Association, 1996).

When full-time nontenurable faculty are hired for their expertise as clinical or research faculty or when they are hired as distinguished senior lecturers, they typically enjoy the perquisites of the tenure-track faculty, with the exception of full voting rights, and are fully integrated into their departments. A few express concern about the lack of job security inherent in renewable appointments; others comment occasionally about status differentials. But these faculty by and large have equivalent credentials to their tenure-track colleagues, have chosen this type of employment, are respected and valued by their colleagues for their expertise, and have the same or very similar employment conditions as the tenure-track faculty. They tend not to be interested in tenure-track positions because they are fully employable in their professions, or have lifestyle concerns that preclude tenure-track appointments. The distinguished senior faculty have enjoyed successful careers outside academe and are not seeking lengthy employment in academe (Gappa, 1996).

The different career paths among the full-time nontenurable faculty make it difficult to interpret data on levels of satisfaction. Of those responding to the NSOPF 1993, most were somewhat or very satisfied with their authority to make decisions about the courses they teach and the noninstructional aspects of their jobs. Three-quarters of the respondents were satisfied with their workload. However, there was less satisfaction with long-term career prospects and ability to keep current in their academic fields. Forty-three percent expressed dissatisfaction with job security, 47 percent with salaries, and 54 percent with opportunities for advancement in rank (National Education Association, 1996). Others expressed resentment about being seen as "second-class citizens" who are denied full opportunities for professional development and participation in governance. Given the wide range of personal circumstances involved one would expect a wide range of reactions from great satisfaction to anger and resentment (Breneman, 1997).

Conclusions and Recommendations

This chapter has briefly described the roles and employment conditions of the new faculty majority: the faculty ineligible for tenure who occupy either full- or part-time positions. Over the past decade, the number of such faculty has increased, while the number in tenure-track or tenured positions has decreased. While the overall satisfaction of part- and full-time non-tenurable faculty is generally high, there is dissatisfaction with working conditions and status.

The idea that tenure is the only way to promote quality is unrealistic in an environment in which the majority of faculty are not eligible for it. As colleges and universities redefine faculty appointments and as increasing numbers of people with more diverse interests, motives, and qualifications enter the academy, it is time to rethink who the faculty are. The new faculty majority includes people with high-level professional experience, cutting-edge clinical and research skills, broad and unusual life experiences, distinguished records of community leadership, perspectives from different cultural points of view, creative and original artistic ideas, experience in politics and government leadership, and a deep and genuine humanity that may not be measurable in conventional terms. Many of these faculty, or prospective faculty, do not consider tenure important (Gappa and Leslie, 1997).

To attract this kind of diverse and high quality faculty, full- and part-time new career paths and more flexibility are essential. Discussions about academic careers can be assisted by looking at modifications and alternatives to traditional tenure that are already occurring within academe and at similar professions outside academe (Trower, 1998). A range of types of appointments that meet the needs of institutions and individuals for flexibility and options are needed. Increasingly faculty and prospective faculty are disenchanted with the rigidities of traditional systems of tenure and pleased with the wider array of career tracks available now to full-time non-tenurable faculty. The availability of career tracks outside the tenure system can lead to far less emphasis upon an individual's track and far more consideration of the individual's contribution to the institution (Gappa, 1996).

We must find ways to extend academic freedom and a reasonable amount of job security to all faculty and write them into faculty employment policies. These reforms and the opening up of governance to include tenure-ineligible faculty members will have the added benefit of helping to eliminate status differentials that persist in the current system. Breneman (1997) has suggested higher salaries for tenure-ineligible, full-time appointments to compensate for the lack of job security, and initial appointments of a duration equal to that of entering tenure-track faculty to avoid status differentials.

Faculty rewards and recognition should be based on productivity rather than on status in a system of tenure. All faculty members should be evaluated and rewarded for their performance. Tying rewards directly to exemplary performance, regardless of time base or career track, can go a long way toward achieving integration and improving quality.

To achieve these goals for part-timers will require the most reform. First, the use of part-time faculty should be based on educational, not fiscal, reasons. Institutions with a clear sense of mission will define the kinds of faculty they want and select the members of that faculty on the basis of their ability to perform, not on full- or part-time status. Second, colleges and universities must develop employment policies and practices to ensure that all part-timers are treated fairly and consistently and given the tools they need to do their jobs. Third, these employment policies and practices should provide for differences among part-time employment from intermittent, temporary use to continuing, extended appointment periods. Finally, part-timers must be oriented and integrated into their departments and institutions as fully participating members of the faculty eligible to participate in faculty development programs and opportunities (Gappa and Leslie, 1997; American Association of State Colleges and Universities, 1999).

All faculty members represent a major capital investment by colleges and universities. Just as buildings and equipment need maintaining and renovating, faculty members need support and opportunities to learn, grow, develop, and renew (Gappa and Leslie, 1997). With an adequate and fair investment of resources, all faculty, part- and full-time, eligible and ineligible for tenure, can work together as one faculty to develop new curricula and ways of teaching, deepen their understanding of the subjects and students they teach, and enhance the overall quality of their colleges and universities.

References

American Association of State Colleges and Universities. "Facing Change: Building the Faculty of the Future." Washington, D.C.: American Association of State Colleges and Universities, 1999.

Benjamin, E. "Variations in the Characteristics of Part-Time Faculty by General Fields of Instruction and Research." In D. W. Leslie (ed.), *The Growing Use of Part-Time*

Faculty: Understanding Causes and Effects. New Directions for Higher Education, no. 104. San Francisco: Jossey-Bass, 1998.

Breneman, D. W. "Alternatives to Tenure for the Next Generation of Academics." AAHE Working Paper Series no. 14. Washington, D.C.: American Association for Higher Education, 1997.

Gappa, J. M. "Off the Tenure Track: Six Models for Full-Time Nontenurable Appointments." AAHE Working Paper Series no. 10. Washington, D.C.: American Association for Higher Education, 1996.

Gappa, J. M., and Leslie, D. W. *The Invisible Faculty.* San Francisco: Jossey-Bass, 1993.

Gappa, J. M., and Leslie, D. W. "Two Faculties or One? The Conundrum of Part-Timers in a Bifurcated Work Force." AAHE Working Paper Series no. 6. Washington, D.C.: American Association for Higher Education, 1997.

Haeger, J. D. "Part-Time Faculty, Quality Programs, and Economic Realities." In D. W. Leslie (ed.), *The Growing Use of Part-Time Faculty: Understanding Causes and Effects.* New Directions for Higher Education, no. 104. San Francisco: Jossey-Bass, 1998.

Jones, R. F., and Sanderson, S. C. "Tenure Policies in U.S. and Canadian Medical Schools." *Academic Medicine,* 1994, 69(9), 772–778.

Leatherman, C. "Growth in Positions off the Tenure Track Is a Trend That's Here to Stay, Study Finds." *Chronicle of Higher Education,* Apr. 9, 1999, pp. A14–A16.

Leslie, D. W. "Part-Time, Adjunct, and Temporary Faculty: The New Majority?" Report of the Sloan Conference on Part-Time and Adjunct Faculty. Williamsburg, Va.: College of William and Mary, 1998a.

Leslie, D. W. "Editor's Notes." In D. W. Leslie (ed.), *The Growing Use of Part-Time Faculty: Understanding Causes and Effects.* New Directions for Higher Education, no. 104. San Francisco: Jossey-Bass, 1998b.

National Education Association. "Full-Time Non-Tenure-Track Faculty." NEA Higher Education Research Center, Occasional Topical Research Report, vol. 2, no. 5. Washington, D.C.: National Education Association, 1996.

Trower, C. A. "Employment Practices in the Professions: Fresh Ideas from Inside and Outside the Academy." AAHE Working Paper Series no. 13. Washington, D.C.: American Association for Higher Education, 1998.

Wilson, R. "Georgia State U. Cuts Some Part-Time Positions to Add 65 Full-Time Faculty Jobs." *Chronicle of Higher Education,* June 11, 1999, p. A18.

Wyles, B. A. "Adjunct Faculty in the Community Colleges: Realities and Challenges." In D. W. Leslie (ed.), *The Growing Use of Part-Time Faculty: Understanding Causes and Effects.* New Directions for Higher Education, no. 104. San Francisco: Jossey-Bass, 1998.

JUDITH M. GAPPA is professor of educational administration at Purdue University, West Lafayette, Indiana.

8

*Classified employees are frequently the first
representatives of the college or university whom
prospective students, parents, and others encounter.
Their frontline position makes them highly important
members of the campus community. This chapter
contends that the satisfaction of classified staff
contributes to productivity and overall institutional
effectiveness.*

The Front Line: Satisfaction of Classified Employees

Karen W. Bauer

Clerical and other support staff members comprise approximately forty percent of the higher education workforce (National Center for Education Statistics, 1997a). Although historically many college employment policies were designed for faculty needs, classified support staff—including technical, skilled crafts, maintenance, but primarily clerical and secretarial—often have different needs and interests from faculty and professional staff members. Very often support staff employees work on the front lines. For example, they are the first point of contact for current students, prospective students, parents, legislative officials, and other constituents. This is especially true for clerical staff, whose attitudes and level of helpfulness can substantially contribute to the constituents' perceptions of the campus climate.

This chapter will focus primarily on classified employee satisfaction, but by necessity will also include two related concepts: employee motivation and workforce commitment. These concepts appear to have a bidirectional relationship: in some instances, employee motivation influences satisfaction or workforce commitment; in other circumstances, employee satisfaction may influence motivation or commitment. Motivation is the internal, psychological force that drives individual behavior. Workforce commitment is the psychological investment in one's employment and is the result of employee satisfaction and motivation.

Employee satisfaction is critical for all segments of the workforce, particularly for those in a frontline position. Research in many occupations consistently points to the positive relationship between employee satisfaction and productivity (Allen, 1996; Bassi and Van Buren (1997); Church, 1995; Laabs, 1998; Sauter, Hurrell, and Cooper, 1989; Savery, 1996). In a review of empirical studies on job satisfaction, Locke (1976) identified seven working conditions associated with job satisfaction:

- Mentally challenging work with which one can successfully cope
- Personal interest in the work itself
- Work that is not too physically tiring
- Rewards for performance
- Good working conditions
- High self-esteem
- Attainment of interesting work, pay, and promotions, and help in minimizing role conflict and ambiguity

Employee satisfaction affects turnover rates. Murray and Murray (1996) reported that turnover in managerial positions can cost an organization from five to twenty-five times an employee's monthly salary including but not limited to downtime for training, orientation to campus, knowledge of campus services, as well as costs associated with time to build rapport with colleagues and supervisor.

Clearly, lower satisfaction influences morale, camaraderie, and performance. In a Gallup Organization survey of more than one hundred thousand employees in large companies over a period of twenty-five years, researchers found that "those units of the company where employees were the happiest were often the most successful" ("It's the Manager, Stupid," 1998, p. 54). Positive relationships with supervisors and coworkers contribute substantially to job satisfaction and performance. In what has been referred to as *value chain* (Vincola and Mobley, 1998) the presence of happy employees increased the likelihood of productive work. This research supports the assumption of strong links between work-life initiatives and performance management. The value chain asserts that if the work environment produces happy, productive, and satisfied employees (the work-life balance) and provides clear expectations for employees (performance management), the results will be efficient and effective productivity. It seems likely, then, that higher education managers should seek to maintain or create a positive value chain.

The Relationship Between Financial Retrenchment and Employee Satisfaction

Financial retrenchment in the early 1990s led to employee downsizing and, in some cases, an increase in the privatization of services. Retrenchment affects all employees but may especially impact classified employees. Exploration of, or actual move to, privatization and layoffs can create low morale, cut productivity, and contribute to overall job dissatisfaction. It is often assumed that elimination of excess processes, goods, and employees can make the company or institution leaner and meaner, thus more productive.

Unfortunately, the connection may not be direct or certain. Interestingly, Bassi and Van Buren (1997) report that fewer than half of the companies downsized between 1990 and 1996 actually had short- or long-term profit increases and even fewer reported increases in employee productivity, product service quality, and shareholder value.

In concert with financial retrenchment, many institutions heightened their emphasis on Total Quality Management (TQM). In the early to mid-1990s, many higher education officials undertook the study and implementation of TQM and similar concepts such as Continuous Quality Initiatives, emphasizing high quality products and outcomes, effective and efficient processing of products, and efforts to ensure customer satisfaction. This inherent principle to ensure customer satisfaction led higher education officials to address so-called customer relations and in particular the interactions of frontline staff such as cashiers, admissions, and financial aid staff with current and prospective students.

Frontline Satisfaction

The literature has identified four key factors that contribute to employee satisfaction and workforce commitment: (1) rewards and recognition, (2) issues of work-life balance, (3) opportunities for growth through training and development, and (4) perceptions of the work environment. Outstanding companies are noted for their insight and attention to these factors and higher education officials are following their lead by addressing these issues for faculty and professional as well as classified employees.

Rewards and Recognition. A great debate rages regarding the importance of intrinsic versus extrinsic rewards. From the limited number of studies available, it appears that satisfaction moves from the extrinsic to the intrinsic as workers age. Thus, younger employees are more motivated by tangible, extrinsic rewards such as salary. Some researchers, such as those who conducted the Workforce Commitment Study (Aon Consulting, 1998) found salary (for 62 percent of the two thousand employees surveyed) and employee benefits (for 57 percent) were the two most important factors attracting and retaining employees.

Other researchers such as Herzberg (1959), Laabs (1998), Leavitt (1996), and Savery (1996) believe that intrinsic factors such as interpersonal relationships, working conditions, status, and security pose a much greater influence on job satisfaction. In addition, although salary is especially important in attracting persons to the job initially, benefits contribute to the employee's length of tenure. The Workforce Commitment Study (Aon Consulting, 1998) found that positive experiences with specific benefits correlate with increased commitment. For example, employer-paid pension plans, employee assistance programs, and flexible work schedules significantly correlated with workforce commitment. It is likely that these factors also affect job satisfaction. Researchers at Aon found retirement programs and work-life programs to have the greatest impact on commitment; prescription drug cards, long-term care insurance, and vision insurance had the least impact.

Other data available for job satisfaction on salary and benefits in higher education is mixed. For example, in a recent survey at Mid-Plains Community College, employees including classified staff reported being the least satisfied with rewards, which included salary and benefits (Ford, 1992). However, in a recent employee satisfaction survey at the University of Delaware, 48 percent of the salaried staff said they were very satisfied with their salary and 93 percent agreed that university benefits are excellent ("University of Delaware Employee Satisfaction Survey Summary," 1996). In this survey, 71 percent of the salaried staff reported being satisfied with their jobs overall.

Personal Choice and Empowerment. The ability to choose among benefits may be an important factor in job satisfaction. Respondents in the Aon study ranked ability to choose benefits that best fit their needs as the fourth most important factor in job satisfaction, following employer-paid pension plans, employee assistance programs, and flexible work schedules. The importance of salary versus benefits may vary for different groups and likely reflects differing needs. For example, the Aon study found employees aged forty and over, as well as married employees without children, reported benefits to be of equal or greater importance than salary (Aon Consulting, 1998).

However, high pay and benefits alone do not ensure satisfaction; attention to career development issues is also important (Leavitt, 1996). Laabs (1998) believes that employee satisfaction and retention can be enhanced when managers demonstrate that employees are needed, valued, and appreciated. All employees appreciate praise—a basic human need—or other recognition for completing their tasks well. Worker appreciation does not necessarily mean additional financial costs. While it may require awareness, thought, and time, the gain in employee performance and morale may be well worth the trouble. Premium parking spots, an office with a window, or specific computer software are often prized commodities that affect satisfaction, and may cost the supervisor little or nothing. Many institutions are currently engaged in employee of the month or merit award programs. Deserving employees may be highlighted in a campus newspaper or Internet article. Presumably, the outcomes of such rewards are increased employee morale, a productive staff, and an increased feeling of community among workers.

Work-Life Balance. As the twenty-first century begins, there is a greater emphasis on balance in life and a resultant increase in research examining the relationship between job and life satisfaction. The baby boomers and Generation X workers have marked the trail for devoting more time to family, leisure, and physical activities. Perhaps more than other workers, classified staff members are often challenged with resolution of tough life issues such as child care or elder care issues.

One issue studied in this area is the direction of the relationship between job and life satisfaction. Although some researchers believe it to be directional (for example, job satisfaction affecting life satisfaction), others have argued that it is reciprocal in nature (Howard and Frink, 1996). It is quite possible that family difficulties at home may add stress, lower motivation or health, and thwart the classified staff member from concentrating on job duties (Hagedorn and Sax, 1999). It is also quite possible, however, that stress or even simple change in the work setting may influence life satisfaction outside the job. Astute campus supervisors are aware of this possible detractor from job productivity and support classified staff members in achieving good work and life balance.

Child Care. Since 88 percent of all clerical and secretarial employees in higher education are female (National Center for Education Statistics, 1997a), it follows that many classified staff members are working mothers. In 1960, fewer than 20 percent of women with children under six years and about 39 percent of women with children six to seventeen years were employed. By 1990, the numbers had rapidly risen to 60 and 75 percent respectively (General Accounting Office, 1992). Marquart (1991) found that users of on-site child care facilities were more likely to work overtime and were likely to be satisfied with their jobs, compared to those who did not have the benefit of on-site child care. Rodgers and Rodgers (1989) found that companies with policies that held little regard for family issues experienced greater turnover and economic losses. In addition, they found that "employees who perceived their supervisors as unsupportive on family issues reported higher levels of stress, greater absenteeism, and lower job satisfaction" (p. 123).

The average U.S. employee misses fifteen days per year, four of which are for personal illness, and eleven for personal and family matters (Aon Consulting, 1998). While some postsecondary institutions offer generous leave policies, many do not reward employees for accrual of large number of sick days. For some, the mentality is, "use it or lose it"—an attitude that may subtly reinforce unnecessary absences. Some institutions have implemented smart policies to discourage sick leave abuse. For example, at retirement, individuals with a large number of sick days accrued may receive credit of additional months or even years in their retirement benefits. Some policies reinforce work attendance in a way that financially benefits the employee, increasing motivation to attend work as well as increasing overall satisfaction.

Quality of child care is also an issue. At an urban college campus, researchers found that type of child care for classified employees was not a significant predictor of absenteeism, but the quality of care was important to satisfaction.

Elder Care. In addition to child care needs, care for elderly parents has placed increased stress on many employees, including clerical workers. Many staff workers are in the so-called sandwich generation, pressed to find adequate care for both aging parents and young children during work hours.

Higher education institutions have taken the lead from a few major companies such as IBM, Johnson and Johnson, Motorola, and MBNA who have implemented flexible family leave policies, on-site child care programs, and greater information about elderly care options. The availability of on-site daycare is often cited as one of the key indicators of the best companies and an issue that can increase employee satisfaction and commitment.

Growth Through Training and Development. Another factor in classified staff satisfaction is the opportunity for growth. Especially in higher education settings, continuing education is easily accessible and often available through tuition discounts or waiver. Many clerical staff earn associate and bachelor's degrees while employed. And if not seeking a full degree, clerical staff are motivated to attend workshops, seminars, and certificate programs, or to update computer and other technology skills. General education, specific academic information, as well as refresher courses or workshops to update word-processing or computer skills are offered frequently and in some cases geared specifically for clerical staff members.

Classified employees' access to training for job duties is high and often used. For example, in a staff survey at Pacific Lutheran University (Fletcher, 1997), 53 percent of the respondents said they needed additional job-related computer training. To meet this type of need, officials in many colleges are offering short, focused workshops to update computer and other technology skills. At the Northwestern Michigan College (NMC) 77 percent of employees have participated in quality training activities (Merrill, 1995). Similarly, 71 percent of the salaried staff who responded to a University of Delaware survey on employee satisfaction said they were given the opportunity to improve skills; two-thirds of the respondents were satisfied with staff training and development (University of Delaware Employee Satisfaction Survey Summary, 1996).

Difficulty may arise when office duties and class workshop time conflict. In most cases, clerical staff is expected to answer telephones and act as the first contact with visitors. Absence for class or training sessions over an extended time period often leaves supervisors without phone or office coverage. This may cause difficulty for supervisors who have to handle those tasks themselves or who choose to divert calls to the answering machine. In high traffic offices, this may extend the appearance that no one is available to help students or prospective students, thus leaving a negative impression. This can be a source of stress for both the supervisor and the clerical staff member, but can be reduced by offering computer training and other workshops at various times to accommodate different schedules.

The benefits derived from increased classified staff training can be well worth the hassles in office coverage. Staff members who perceive growth opportunities are more satisfied (Howard and Frink, 1996). Not only will classified staff members be learning skills that directly affect their daily competency, but they will also gain the indirect benefits of increased self-esteem and empowerment.

Employee Perceptions of Working Conditions and the Work Environment

Regardless of salary and benefits, total work-life balance, and opportunities for training, one's perceptions of the specific work situation will strongly affect the perceived level of job satisfaction. Several factors contribute to individual perceptions, including interpersonal relationships with coworkers, perceptions of campus multiculturalism, internal motivation, involvement in decision-making, and perceptions of the physical work environment.

Interpersonal Relationships with Coworkers. Friendly (but professional) relationships with coworkers are important for classified employees' job satisfaction. Social support at work satisfies a human need for companionship and group affiliation (Jahoda, 1982) and serves as a resource to moderate the impact of job demands (House, 1981). Howard and Frink (1996) found that satisfaction with coworkers has a positive relationship with both internal work motivation and general job satisfaction, and Allen (1996) found that the quality of coworker and employee-supervisor communication was directly related to voluntary turnover intentions. Whether held around the office watercooler, during lunchtime, or at a staff meeting, conversations contribute to a support network that may help workers deal effectively with daily work demands (National Initiative for Leadership and Institutional Effectiveness, 1998).

In addition to increasing worker satisfaction, positive social relationships among staff members may also contribute to better health. Some researchers believe that friendly coworker relationships produce a "buffering effect" and that social support is a "significant factor in lowering the impact and perceived stress and job strain on physical and mental health" (Johnson, 1989; Sauter, Hurrell, and Cooper, 1989, p. 65).

To address these needs many college and university managers coordinate staff retreats or other team-building exercises. Many institutions offer a variety of stress reduction or other health-related programs for employees. Friendly support of coworkers and knowledge of stress reduction techniques may increase job satisfaction and work productivity.

Perceptions of Campus Multiculturalism. Perceptions of campus multiculturalism affects all members of the campus community but may impact frontline staff significantly more. In 1993, minorities comprised approximately 29 percent of all college classified staff and only 14 percent of executive, managerial, and administrative staff (National Center for Education Statistics, 1997b). To address issues of multiculturalism, many campuses have formed campus-wide committees on multiculturalism. Among those examining racial climate are the San Diego Community College District (SDCCD) and Prince George's Community College (PGCC) in Maryland. In the 1995 SDCCD survey of classified staff, the majority (79 percent) of respondents said they believed there was a positive climate for racial and ethnic diversity. Although most (67 percent) felt that subtle discrimination was dealt with directly and immediately by administrators, approximately one-fifth reported they had been occasionally or frequently discriminated against because of their race, ethnicity, or gender.

Clearly, it is important that campus administrators regularly monitor classified staff perceptions of the environment. Often, classified employees are treated differently from faculty and professional staff, and they may experience and report perceptions of the environment that differ from other campus employees. The 1992 survey of racial climate at PGCC revealed striking differences in perceptions between faculty and staff. Faculty members were the most optimistic about campus relations while staff were the most concerned (Boughan, 1992). Further, although 38 percent of the staff rated race relations as good or better, 15 percent rated them as poor.

Minority classified staff may experience and report additional perceptions of bias or discrimination. In a survey on attitudes toward women and ethnic minorities at San Joaquin Delta College, classified staff (regardless of race), African Americans, and Hispanics (regardless of position) were more likely to give negative responses than managers, men, and full-time faculty (Debow-Makino and others, 1993).

Physical Work Environment. Proper lighting, temperature, air circulation, work-related equipment, and allotted space are related to job satisfaction. As frontline classified employees often come in contact with current and prospective students, it is important that they be given proper equipment and training that enables them to complete job tasks quickly and accurately. Replacement of old computer or other equipment is not only efficient for completion of daily tasks, but can also serve as one of the noncash rewards to recognize classified staff members' positive contributions.

Inherent in some of the grand old institutional buildings that were built many years ago are concerns about health issues such as asbestos, radon gas emission, and lead in drinking water. With lower status than other college employees, classified staff members may be assigned less desirable working spaces. Their concerns about the physical environment, if not addressed, can quickly diminish their job satisfaction and motivation.

Employee Involvement in Decision-Making. Employees report increased satisfaction and commitment when they perceive themselves as members of a good working team involved in decision making. Sauter, Hurrell and Cooper (1989) report a statistically significant relationship between employee participation in decision-making and satisfaction ($r = .36$). Summarizing the research on employee participation, these authors report that participation in decision-making explains approximately 10 to 15 percent of the variance in measures of job satisfaction and about 5 percent of the variance in self-reported mental and physical health outcomes.

Locke and Schweiger (1979) believe that the relationship between participation and employee satisfaction is stronger than the relationship between participation and job performance. The strength of the relationship between participation and satisfaction may depend on whether the involvement is voluntary or forced. When classified staff make suggestions and offer feedback, they feel included, respected, and valued. This, in turn, increases satisfaction as well as other positive outcomes such as institutional loyalty and productivity.

Differences in Job Satisfaction by Personal Demographics. In general, most employees in higher education report high levels of satisfaction, but findings by age and gender are mixed. Vander Putten, McLendon, and Peterson (1997) found many significant differences between work environment indices (for example, emphasis on continuous improvement, unit support, overall performance) and age, race, and educational level. Similarly, Howard and Frink (1996) found that both level of education, age, experience, and level in the organization's hierarchy affect job satisfaction. These findings have clear implications for classified staff who are often the group of employees with lower levels of education, experience, pay, and location in the hierarchy.

Kacmar and Ferris (1989) and Likert (in Savery, 1996) reported that the relationship between age and job satisfaction is curvilinear (U-shaped): satisfaction for young employees is high, falls when individuals are in their 20s and 30s, and then increases again with age. Savery (1996) also reports that women, in general, are less likely to be satisfied with their jobs than men. This finding "may be due to the lack of challenge in women's jobs . . . or to the poor success to date in opening up management and corporate boards to women." (p. 19). Others (Lee and Wilbur, 1985; Rhodes, 1983) found a positive linear relationship between satisfaction and age.

Summary

Classified staff form approximately 40 percent of the workforce in institutions of higher education, and often work on the front lines as the first contact with current and prospective students. Their job satisfaction and consequent productivity should be a high priority to managers and supervisors.

Key factors that contribute to classified staff satisfaction are rewards and recognition; work-life balance; opportunities for growth; training and development; and perceptions of the work environment. Along with the need to inform current and potential students that their needs are important, so too must managers address the needs of classified staff. The evidence appears to indicate that attention to staff needs will result in positive outcomes such as satisfaction and productivity. Rewards and recognition, opportunities for feedback, and help with achieving a healthy work-life balance are likely to enable employees to feel valued and satisfied. In turn, employees who feel valued by their institution will most likely be more satisfied and may also be more loyal and productive.

References

Allen, M. W. "The Relationship Between Communication, Affect, Job Alternatives, and Voluntary Turnover." *Southern Communication Journal,* 1996, *61*(3), 198–209.

Aon Consulting. "America at Work: The Workforce Commitment Study." [http://www.aon.com/prodserv/consulting/atwork/work_1998surv]. 1998.

Bassi, L. J., and Van Buren, M. E. "Sustaining High Performance in Bad Times." *Training and Development,* 1997, *51*(6), 32–41.

Boughan, K. *Employee Perceptions of the Racial Climate at Prince George's Community College.* Prince George's Community College Research Report. Largo, Md.: Prince George's Community College, 1992. (ED 352 106)

Church, A. H. "Managerial Behaviors and Work Group Climate as Predictors of Employee Outcomes." *Human Resource Development Quarterly,* 1995, *6*(2), 173–205.

Debow-Makino, G., and others. "Attitudes on Staff Participation and the Acceptance of Women and Minorities at Delta College: Results of a Staff Opinion Survey Made in Response to an Accreditation Report Recommendation." Research report, 1993. Available from the ERIC Document Reproduction Service, (800) 443-ERIC. (ED 374 842)

Fletcher, K. "1997–98 Pacific Lutheran University Staff Survey Summary Report." Tacoma, Wash.: Office of Institutional Research and Assessment, Pacific Lutheran University, 1997.

Ford, C. *Report of Organizational MPCCA Climate Survey.* North Platte, Nebr.: Mid-Plains Community College, 1992. (ED 349 050)

General Accounting Office. "The Changing Work Force: Comparison of Federal and Nonfederal Work/Family Programs and Approaches." Washington, D.C.: Government Printing Office, 1992.

Hagedorn, L. S., and Sax, L. J. "Marriage, Children, and Aging Parents: The Role of Family-Related Factors in Faculty Job Satisfaction." Paper presented at the American Educational Research Association, Montreal, Canada, Apr. 1999.

Herzberg, F. *The Motivation to Work.* New York: Wiley, 1959.

House, J. *Work Stress and Social Support.* Reading, Mass.: Addison Wesley, 1981.

Howard, J. L., and Frink, D. D. "The Effects of Organizational Restructure on Employee Satisfaction." *Group and Organizational Management,* 1996, *21*(3), 278–303.

"It's the Manager, Stupid." *Economist,* 1998, *348,* 54.

Jahoda, M. *Employment and Unemployment: A Social-Psychological Analysis.* New York: Cambridge University Press, 1982.

Johnson, J. V. "Control, Collectivity, and the Psychosocial Work Environment." In S. L. Sauter, J. J. Hurrell, Jr., and C. L. Cooper (eds.), *Job Control and Worker Satisfaction.* New York: Wiley, 1989.

Kacmar, K. M., and Ferris, G. R. "Theoretical and Methodological Considerations in the Age-Job Satisfaction Relationship." *Journal of Applied Psychology,* 1989, *74,* 201–207.

Laabs, J. "Satisfy Them with More Than Money." *Workforce,* Nov. 1998, 77.

Leavitt, W. M. "High Pay and Low Morale—Can High Pay, Excellent Benefits, Job Security, and Low Job Satisfaction Coexist in a Public Agency?" *Public Personnel Management,* 1996, *25*(3), 333–341.

Lee, R., and Wilbur, E. R. "Age, Education, Job Tenure, Salary, Job Characteristics, and Job Satisfaction: A Multivariate Analysis." *Human Relations,* 1985, *38,* 781–791.

Locke, E. A. "The Nature and Causes of Job Satisfaction." In M. D. Dunnette (ed.), *Handbook of Industrial and Organizational Psychology.* Chicago: Rand McNally, 1976.

Locke, E. A., and Schweiger, D. M. "Participation in Decision-Making: One More Look." In B. M. Staw (ed.), *Research in Organizational Behavior.* Vol. 1. Greenwich, Conn.: JAI Press, 1979.

Marquart, J. "How Does the Employer Benefit from Child Care?" In J. S. Hyde and M. J. Essex (eds.), *Parental Leave and Child Care.* Philadelphia: Temple University Press, 1991.

Merrill, S., and others. "Quality Culture: NMC Ends Report." Traverse City: North-western Michigan College, Aug. 1995. (ED 387 161)

Murray, J., and Murray, J. "Job Dissatisfaction and Turnover Among Two-Year College Department/Division Chairpersons." Proceedings of the annual international conference of National Community College Chair Academy, Phoenix, Ariz., Feb. 1996.

National Center for Education Statistics. "Digest of Education Statistics 1997: Table 222." [http://nces.ed.gov/pubs/digest97/d97t222.html]. 1997a.

National Center for Education Statistics. "Digest of Education Statistics 1997: Table 223." [http://nces.ed.gov/pubs/digest97/d97t223.html]. 1997b.

National Initiative for Leadership and Institutional Effectiveness. [http://www2.ncsu.edu/ncsu/cep/acce/nilie/pub_abs.html]. 1998.

Rhodes, S. R. "Age-Related Differences in Work Attitudes and Behavior: A Review and Conceptual Analysis." *Psychological Bulletin*, 1983, *93,* 328–367.

Rodgers, F. S., and Rodgers, C. "Business and the Facts of Family Life." *Harvard Business Review,* 1989, *67,* 121–129.

Sauter, S. L., Hurrell, J. J., Jr., and Cooper, C. L. *Job Control and Worker Health.* New York: Wiley, 1989.

Savery, L. K. "The Congruence Between the Importance of Job Satisfaction and Perceived Level of Achievement." *Journal of Management Development,* 1996, *15*(6), 18–28.

"University of Delaware Employee Satisfaction Survey Summary." Office of Institutional Research and Planning. Newark: University of Delaware, 1996.

Vander Putten, J., McLendon, M., and Peterson, M. "Comparing Union and Nonunion Staff Perceptions of the Higher Education Work Environment." *Research in Higher Education,* 1997, *38*(1), 131–149.

Vincola, A., and Mobley, N. "Performance Management Through a Work/Life Lens." *HR Focus,* 1998, *75*(2), 9–11.

KAREN W. BAUER is assistant director of institutional research and planning and assistant professor of psychology and women's studies at the University of Delaware. She serves as a faculty member at the AIR Foundations Institute and is the 1998–99 president of the North East Association for Institutional Research.

9

This chapter provides a review of the literature on the factors that influence job satisfaction, life satisfaction, inter-role conflict, and stress of student affairs administrators. Implications for practice are also discussed.

Factors That Influence Satisfaction for Student Affairs Administrators

Janet E. Anderson, Florence Guido-DiBrito, Jean Schober Morrell

For many workers, work and nonwork activities are interdependent (Greenhaus, Bedeian, and Mossholder, 1987). These blurred boundaries may be even more permeable for student affairs administrators, professionals who attend to the services needed by college students such as financial aid, admissions, housing, among others and who attend to the development of residence life, academic and career advising, and multicultural centers (Rentz and Assocs., 1996). Unfortunately, "the work culture in many student affairs organizations is one that demands long hours of hard work for levels of compensation that are not competitive with the private sector" (Nobbe and Manning, 1997, p. 108). Demanding schedules and work overload may frequently be responsible for interpersonal and time conflicts which can reduce job satisfaction and increase stress. Thus, job dissatisfaction and stress may play a role in the level of satisfaction an administrator receives from life in general.

Most U.S. citizens are generally satisfied with their jobs and their lives (Hugick and Leonard, 1991). Yet there has been very little research focused exclusively on student affairs administrators. Additionally, there is a dearth of research on the stress and inter-role conflict levels of these professionals. Ann Austin (1984) has indicated that the higher education workplace is no longer an idyllic state: "For many years, the quality of worklife (sic) in universities and colleges has been viewed as ideal compared to working conditions in other settings. However, higher education is now experiencing pressures from several directions—declining economic resources, low mobility in the academic marketplace, greater centralization of decision-making—which may alter its assumed advantages for the people working within it" (p. 1). Factors especially pertinent to student affairs workers—such as decreased job security, less flexibility, lack of time, a changing work environment, and too much work for one person to complete—negatively affect the stress level of student affairs administrators (Bender, 1980; Morrell, 1994).

This chapter provides a review of the literature on the job satisfaction, life satisfaction, inter-role conflict, and stress level of student affairs administrators from the entry-level to senior student affairs officer (SSAO). Literature from studies conducted using academic administrators and other populations in and out of the academy is woven throughout for comparison. The chapter concludes with implications and suggestions for how student affairs and higher education administrators may address the pertinent issues discussed.

Job Satisfaction

A study of job satisfaction among the general population finds that 83 percent of U.S. workers report general satisfaction with their jobs (Hugick and Leonard, 1991). Although the satisfaction level among administrators is reported to be essentially the same as for workers in other business settings (Boone, 1986), evidence suggests that faculty and administrators in higher education may be less satisfied in their jobs than the general population (Glick, 1992; Solomon and Tierney, 1977). Because so few studies have been conducted using student affairs administrators as subjects, we also examined the job satisfaction literature related to academic affairs administrators to deepen our understanding of job satisfaction for all higher education administrators.

Academic and Other Higher Education Administrators. Much of the research on job satisfaction for higher education administrators examined the differences between women and men and administrator differences by institutional type. Regrettably, results of studies on job satisfaction were less encouraging for women faculty and administrators than for men (Reisser and Zurfluh, 1987; Steward and others, 1995). However, female academic administrators with advanced degrees reported more job satisfaction than women administrators with only a bachelor's degree (Reeves, 1975). Married female administrators were more satisfied with their jobs than their single female counterparts (Reeves, 1975). Women university academic and career administrators with Ph.D.'s reported the highest satisfaction with their role and occupation (Schonwetter, Bond, and Perry, 1993). Although significant differences were found between the four groups studied, in descending order of reported satisfaction were: women with Ph.D.'s, men with Ph.D.'s, men without Ph.D.'s, and women without Ph.D's. Thus, it appears that increased education and experience produce greater job satisfaction, especially for women.

Upper-level administrators in private institutions of higher education were very satisfied with most areas of their jobs (Solomon and Tierney, 1977)—more satisfied than their counterparts in public higher education (Reisser and Zurfluh, 1987). At private institutions, senior administrators reported higher levels of satisfaction than mid-level administrators. However, a study of women in higher education at all administrative levels in the state of Washington revealed different results (Reisser and Zurfluh, 1987). Seventy-eight percent reported serious thoughts of resigning, with external factors (institutional) contributing to a significant number of women reporting very low levels of job satisfaction. Furthermore, when measured against male administrators in comparable positions, women administrators were significantly less satisfied than men (Zurfluh and Reisser, 1990).

A study of academic administrators selected from a large population of four-year colleges and universities concluded "that academic administrators at four-year institutions of higher education perceive dissatisfaction in the nature of the work they are required to perform" (Glick, 1992, p. 632). The job satisfaction mean score for these administrators was above the normed mean score on four of the five variables of the Job Descriptive Index. However, when compared with normative data for administrators with similar educational levels, the subjects in this study reported slightly lower levels of job satisfaction.

Student Affairs Administrators. Using a random sample of professionals from various administrative levels and all institutional types, Bender (1980) performed one of the first studies focusing exclusively on job satisfaction in student affairs. Bender found no differences by gender or age in the level of satisfaction. The study concluded that "while 66 percent of the sample indicated that they were satisfied with their jobs, and 16 percent indicated that they were undecided, only 18 percent of the respondents reported job dissatisfaction at the current time" (p. 4).

Given the low status of student affairs as a profession in the higher education administrative hierarchy (Bloland, Stamatakos, and Rogers, 1994), it is not surprising that presidents and academic affairs officers reported higher levels of satisfaction with their jobs than their student affairs counterparts (Solomon and Tierney, 1977). A recent national study using a sample of female and male SSAOs revealed age, marital status, and gender determined job satisfaction (Anderson, 1998). This study found a significant contrast between older, married, male SSAOs' high level of job satisfaction and younger, unmarried, female SSAOs' low level of job satisfaction. Specifically, the study revealed male SSAOs were more satisfied with their jobs than female SSAOs; older SSAOs were more satisfied than younger SSAOs; and married SSAOs were more satisfied than unmarried SSAOs.

Shedding light on institutional type and age difference in job satisfaction, another study of student affairs and academic affairs administrators found a positive relationship between job satisfaction and internal locus of control (Tarver, Canada, and Lim, 1999). A positive relationship was found for administrators at all kinds of institutions except at community colleges where a negative relationship existed. A stronger relationship existed between job satisfaction and internal locus of control for older student affairs administrators when compared to younger student affairs administrators and older and younger academic affairs administrators.

Anderson's (1998) findings contradicted earlier studies which looked at academic affairs administrators (for example, Solomon and Tierney, 1977). She found SSAOs who work at public institutions showed slightly higher levels of job satisfaction than those who worked at private institutions (Anderson, 1998). On the other hand, supporting previous research, one recent study demonstrated that "entry-level professionals are among the least satisfied with their positions [in] the student affairs profession" (Blackhurst, Brandt, and Kalinowski, 1998a, p. 29). Focusing on women at all levels of student affairs administration, this study revealed that women at the SSAO or director level were the most satisfied in their administrative role. Women administrators who held associate or assistant SSAO positions had the lowest levels of job satisfaction. Female SSAOs at community colleges were less satisfied with their jobs than those at research institutions (Anderson, 1998).

Life Satisfaction

A study of general life satisfaction found that 88 percent of U.S. workers were satisfied with their lives (Hugick and Leonard, 1991). In general, certain factors appeared to increase life satisfaction including being married (Andrews and Withey, 1976; Crohan, Antonnucci, Adelmann, and Coleman, 1989; Diener, 1984) and older (Diener, 1984). Thus, the fact that women administrators in higher education are more often single or divorced (Bird, 1984) may have implications for their life satisfaction.

As with the job satisfaction research, gender and age appeared to play a role in the life satisfaction of student affairs administrators. Male SSAOs were significantly more satisfied with their lives than female SSAOs (Anderson, 1998). Senior student affairs officers who worked in public institutions were more satisfied with their lives than those who worked in private settings. Age and marital status were also significant factors in that older SSAOs were more satisfied than younger ones, and married SSAOs were more satisfied with their lives than those who never married. These findings appear to support research conducted on the general population.

Place in the administrative hierarchy may also play a role in the life satisfaction of SSAOs. For example, a study found that female SSAOs were statistically more satisfied with their lives than those at lower levels in the organization (Blackhurst, Brandt, and Kalinowski, 1998a). Women at the director's level had more life satisfaction than those at an assistant or associate director's level. Contrary to other research, there was no evidence to suggest that age, number of years in higher education, educational level, or length of time in current position individually influenced life satisfaction. However, the interaction between life satisfaction and position or length of time in higher education did produce significant results. Results indicated that "SSAOs who had been in higher education for more than twenty years reported greater satisfaction with their lives than women in any other group, followed closely by directors who had been in higher education for twenty years or more" (p. 28).

The Job Satisfaction–Life Satisfaction Relationship

The introduction of a meta-analysis review of job satisfaction–life satisfaction studies explains why these two constructs are related (Tait, Padgett, and Baldwin, 1989): "It is generally assumed that job and life satisfaction should be related to one another because, for many people, work is a significant and central aspect of their life (in terms of both time and emotional involvement). As a result, people are believed to have a difficult time separating their feelings about work and life in general, a tendency that is heightened by the importance attached to work in American society" (p. 502). The relationship between job satisfaction and life satisfaction has been studied extensively in the general population for the last thirty years. However, only one study in the student affairs literature addressed this issue, whereas several examined the relationship of job and life satisfaction for faculty.

Both aspects of work and life outside of work were related to job satisfaction and, likewise, work and nonwork conditions were associated with life satisfaction for faculty members (Near and Sorcinelli, 1986). Faculty members tended to experience a high degree of spillover between work and life away from work. In one study, a strong correlation ($r = .64, p < .01$) between job satisfaction and life satisfaction for faculty members is at least two times stronger than the average correlation reported for the public at large ($r = .31, p < .001$) (Rice, Near, and Hunt, 1980). Furthermore, the high prestige status of faculty may influence the high job and life satisfaction of these workers (Near and Sorcinelli, 1986). Moreover, "unlike other respondents, for academics, work appears quite strongly to influence and be influenced by the nature of life outside of work" (p. 388).

For SSAOs, a positive relationship exists between job satisfaction and life satisfaction (Anderson, 1998). In this study, the strongest relationship between these two variables for all respondents ($r = .60, p < .001$) was also the strongest relationship when looking at female respondents alone.

Inter-Role Conflict. The connection between work and nonwork domains suggests that these two areas compete for time and energy (Loscocco and Roschelle, 1991). Often this competition for individual limited resources leads to inter-role conflict between work and life domains.

A study conducted using male and female administrators at all hierarchical levels in all functional areas of higher education found that women reported significantly more time conflicts than men in professional activities (Bird, 1984). Likewise, gender differences were found in the use of role-management strategies, some dimensions of task sharing, and sex-role orientation. The men in this study reported that their family structure allowed for more accommodation of their professional role: 55 percent were married to women who did not work or who worked part-time.

Dual-career couples who worked at Brown University participated in a study which found that women felt more pressured to complete tasks well (for example, tasks related to their many roles as parent, spouse, and worker) than did men (Weishaar, Chiaravalli, and Jones, 1984). Paradoxically, women in this study reported more satisfaction with a family and career combination than men. In fact, women were "more satisfied than men, unless they had children. The only respondents who reported any dissatisfaction were women with children" (p. 19). The negative effects of inter-role conflict may plague women with children and cause low levels of both life and job satisfaction.

One study looking at SSAOs exclusively revealed that female SSAOs reported significantly higher levels of inter-role conflict than male SSAOs ($F = 10.53, P < .0014$) (Anderson, 1998). Qualitative data from the study supported the quantitative findings which revealed that more female respondents were willing to discuss difficulty managing both job and life. The women in this study wrote about sacrificing personal relationships, the failure of relationships because of time spent on the job, and regrets associated with some of their choices to put their career first.

Role Conflict and Job-Life Satisfaction in Higher Education. The relationship between role conflict and job satisfaction among new student affairs professionals may have a negative correlation ($r = -.33$) (Ward, 1995). A slightly higher negative relationship between job satisfaction and role conflict ($r = -.37$) was reported for SSAOs (Anderson, 1998). The negative relationships between role conflict and job satisfaction among all levels of student affairs administrators supported an earlier study illuminating similar results (Solomon and Tierney, 1977).

High levels of role conflict were negatively related to life satisfaction ($r = -.28$) for female student affairs administrators (Blackhurst, Brandt, and Kalinowski, 1998b). Other results supported this finding for female SSAOs ($r = -.46$) (Anderson, 1998). Male SSAOs in Anderson's study also had high levels of role conflict and low job satisfaction, but the relationship was not as strong ($r = -.35$).

Stress

Most of the studies on stress in higher education focus on faculty. In general, faculty report stress derived from high self-expectations, intrafaculty relations, and from time and resource constraints (Carnegie Foundation, 1985; Richard, 1987; Seldin, 1987; Thoreson, Kardash, Leuthold, and Morrow, 1990; Witt and Lovrich, 1988). In studying faculty gender differences as they relate to stress, female faculty report experiencing more stress than male faculty (Witt and Lovrich, 1988; Brown and others, 1986a, 1986b;

Thoreson, Kardash, Leuthold, and Morrow, 1990). The few studies to focus on stress among student affairs administrators reveal similar results (Berwick, 1992; Brown and others, 1986a, 1986b; Morrell, 1994; Scott, 1992; Skipper, 1992). Stress for both genders tends to result from discrepancies between individual and institutional priorities or role conflict.

A study of the stress of student affairs administrators found similar gender differences—with women more stressed than men (Scott and Spooner, 1989). For women, both home and work produced major stress. At the top of the stressor list for female student affairs administrators were divorce, death, or serious illness of a family member or friend, major increase in the amount or pace of work, and too much work or too little time. For men, the stressors were almost exclusively work related including change in position, too much work or too little time, major restructuring of the department or organization, and divorce. Thus, women administrators had unique stressors which influenced the level of stress experienced in the workplace.

A study among student affairs middle managers in the state of Colorado found that the primary stressors were too much work, lack of time, and change in work environment (such as a new supervisor or a major restructuring) (Morrell, 1994). Female student affairs middle managers in this study indicated higher levels of stress at work and away from work than their male counterparts. Stressors away from work were frequently related to caregiving activities and health concerns with children, aging parents, or friends.

Stress is also related to job satisfaction. A study of student affairs professionals in four-year and comprehensive institutions in Minnesota finds that the more satisfied an administrator is in the job, the less stress he or she experiences (Berwick, 1992). The study also reveals that "the lack of time available for family, leisure, and research activities may be contributing to individuals' job dissatisfaction" (p. 17).

Finally, job satisfaction for administrators is strongly correlated with interpersonal stress and teamwork (Volkwein, Malik, and Napierski-Prancl, 1998): "Stress is associated with low satisfaction, while teamwork is associated with high satisfaction. Their influence is so pervasive that their influence on overall administrative satisfaction is two or three times greater than perceptions about workload and an overly controlled [amount of external regulation] work environment" (p. 58).

Implications for Student Affairs and Higher Education

Low levels of job-life satisfaction at all levels of the profession and high levels of inter-role conflict and stress often lead to health problems for administrators and can be costly to institutions. Certainly, the physical and psychological health of all administrators should be a top priority at all institutions of higher education. In the book *Toxic Work*, Reinhold writes of the connections between work and health: "doing a good job and being appreciated for it builds self-esteem and sense of purpose, which in turn enhances functioning of the cardiovascular and immune systems. Many studies show that work satisfaction increases both health and longevity" (1996, p. 6). Employees who experience negative health consequences are a financial burden on an institution of higher education. Decreased worker productivity and increased absenteeism may result from low job satisfaction and high stress. Additionally, low job satisfaction is associated with high worker turnover (Bender, 1980; Glick, 1992; Murray and Murray, 1998), and low organizational commitment (Blackhurst, Brandt, and Kalinowski, 1998a). Other alternatives must be explored to meet the challenges that lie ahead in light of these costly factors to higher education.

Restructuring the work environment to allow for more flexibility may be one way to reduce stress and enhance productivity for student affairs administrators. Options such as flextime, part-time work, and job sharing may allow administrators more time to devote energy to family concerns such as caring for children or aging parents. Additionally, more realistic job expectations, including realistic time demands, may increase the job satisfaction levels and reduce the amount of inter-role conflict and stress experienced by all administrators. If the demands of the job for student affairs administrators are internally driven, levels of satisfaction may increase and corresponding inter-role conflict and stress may decrease.

Traditionally, men outnumber women in the SSAO position. However, the number of women in student affairs administration positions is increasing. A better understanding of women's work experience in higher education may help counter their higher attrition rate compared to men in the academy (Burns, 1982; Sagaria, 1986). Additionally, "women continue to advance much less quickly than men, have lower average salaries than men, and are in less prestigious fields of study and academic institutions" (Hersi, 1993, p. 29). Female administrators also are more likely to be single than male administrators (Bird, 1984; Reeves, 1975; Scott and Spooner, 1989). These factors contribute to our understanding of why women experience less job and life satisfaction, more inter-role conflict, and more stress.

A myth exists about "women who hold policy-making positions in an institution of higher education [—that they] generally are required by society to be model mothers and spouses, concerned citizens involved in civic activities, good teachers, authors of renown, and exceptional managers" (Villadsen and Tack, 1981, p. 22). These expectations place a heavy burden on women administrators who may determine themselves unworthy of the challenge and choose not to enter higher education administration.

Another way to raise student affairs administrators' productivity and lower their stress is to develop recruitment and hiring policies responsive to student affairs professionals' needs. Policies that are responsive to changing administrator needs may include those for dual-career families and new parents (Hensel, 1991). Family leave policies, including maternity leave, also may be reexamined. In addition, counseling or support groups for dealing with life and work stress issues are important. However, perhaps more important is an organizational climate which encourages and supports participation in these groups. One example is to give all university employees leave time as needed to participate in such a worthwhile activity. College and university employee assistance programs can be helpful to facilitate reduction in stress and role conflict for both male and female administrators and increase their job-life satisfaction.

We must revisit reward structures in student affairs. More than SSAOs, student affairs middle managers indicate higher stress levels from insufficient rewards (Morrell, 1994; Scott, 1992). Furthermore, rewards such as pay, benefits, and recognition are important factors in job satisfaction. SSAOs must ensure that appropriate salary and other reward systems are in place to ensure equity and fairness throughout the student affairs division. In an era of tight fiscal resources, forms of rewards other than pay or benefits are crucial to a healthy student affairs organization.

Given the financial crisis facing higher education and increased demands for accountability, activities to assist student affairs and higher education administrators foster and embrace change may be beneficial (Munz, 1995). As change is needed, it is critical to have staff involved in these decisions (Iannello, 1992). In-service training and professional development opportunities related to time management techniques, technology related to service delivery and student development, and leadership skills—including community building and conflict resolution—for a diverse staff may be helpful as budgets are cut and staff are reduced.

The need to look at the nature of work for student affairs administrators and their satisfaction is critical. With the current booming economy, the profession may be losing well-qualified individuals who opt out of student affairs work because of the factors mentioned in this chapter. Many of these problems can be addressed only if the academy deems them worthy.

References

Anderson, J. E. "A Comparison of Female and Male Senior Student Affairs Officers' Job Satisfaction, Life Satisfaction, and Inter-Role Conflict." Unpublished doctoral dissertation, Department of Educational Leadership and Policy Studies, University of Northern Colorado, 1998.

Andrews, F. M., and Withey, S. B. *Social Indicators of Well-Being: America's Perception of Life Quality.* New York: Plenum, 1976.

Austin, A. E. "Work Orientation of University Mid-Level Administrators: Commitment to Work Role, Institution, and Career." Paper presented at the Association for the Study of Higher Education, Chicago, Mar. 1984.

Bender, B. E. "Job Satisfaction in Student Affairs." *NASPA Journal,* 1980, *18*(2), 2–9.

Berwick, K. R. "Stress Among Student Affairs Administrators: The Relationship of Personal Characteristics and Organizational Variables to Work-Related Stress." *Journal of College Student Development,* 1992, *33,* 11–19.

Bird, G. W. "Family and Career Characteristics of Women and Men College and University Administrators." *Journal of the National Association for Women Deans, Administrators, and Counselors,* 1984, *47*(4), 21–28.

Blackhurst, A. E., Brandt, J. E., and Kalinowski, J. "Effects of Career Development on the Organizational Commitment and Life Satisfaction of Women Student Affairs Administrators." *NASPA Journal,* 1998a, *36,* 19–34.

Blackhurst, A. E., Brandt, J. E., and Kalinowski, J. "Effects of Personal and Work-Related Attributes on the Organizational Commitment and Life Satisfaction of Women Student Affairs Administrators." *NASPA Journal,* 1998b, *35,* 86–99.

Bloland, P. A., Stamatakos, L. C., and Rogers, R. R. *Reform in Student Affairs: A Critique of Student Development.* Greensboro, N.C.: ERIC Counseling and Student Services Clearinghouse, 1994.

Boone, C. W. "The Relationships Between Job Characteristics, Role Conflict, Role Ambiguity, Internal Locus of Control, and Job Satisfaction of College and University Administrators." Doctoral dissertation, University of Denver, 1986. Abstract in *Dissertation Abstracts International,* 47(1986).

Brown, R. D., and others. "Stress on Campus: An Interactional Perspective." *Research in Higher Education,* 1986a, *24*(1), 97–112.

Brown, R. D., and others. "Studying Stress Among Student Services Professionals: An Interactional Approach." *NASPA Journal,* 1986b, *23*(4), 2–10.

Burns, M. A. "Who Leaves the Student Affairs Field?" *NASPA Journal,* 1982, *20*(2), 9–12.

Carnegie Foundation. "Survey of College Faculty: The Faculty Deeply Troubled." *Change,* 1985, *4, 31*–34.

Crohan, S. E., Antonnucci, T. C., Adelmann, P. K., and Coleman, L. M. "Job Characteristics and Well-Being at Midlife." *Psychology of Women Quarterly,* 1989, *13,* 223–235.

Diener, E. "Subjective Well-Being." *Psychological Bulletin,* 1984, *95,* 542–575.

Glick, N. L. "Job Satisfaction Among Academic Administrators." *Research in Higher Education,* 1992, *33,* 625–639.

Greenhaus, J. H., Bedeian, A. G., and Mossholder, K. W. "Work Experiences, Job Performance, and Feelings of Personal and Family Well-Being." *Journal of Vocational Behavior,* 1987, *31,* 200–215.

Hensel, N. *Realizing Gender Equality in Higher Education: The Need to Integrate Work/Family Issues.* ASHE-ERIC Higher Education Report no. 2. Washington, D.C.: George Washington University, 1991.

Hersi, D. T. "Factors Contributing to Job Satisfaction for Women in Higher Education Administration." *CUPA Journal,* 1993, *44*(2), 29–35.

Hugick, L., and Leonard, J. "Job Dissatisfaction Grows: 'Moonlighting' on the Rise." *Gallup Poll News Service,* 1991, *56,* 1–11.

Iannello, K. P. *Feminist Interventions in Organization Theory and Practice.* New York: Routledge, 1992.

Loscocco, K. A., and Roschelle, A. E. "Influences on the Quality of Work and Nonwork Life: Two Decades in Review." *Journal of Vocational Behavior,* 1991, *39,* 182–225.

Morrell, J. S. "Sources of Stress for the Student Affairs Mid-Manager." Unpublished doctoral dissertation, Department of Educational Leadership and Policy Studies, University of Northern Colorado, 1994.

Munz, D. C. "Helping Employees Manage the Stress of Working in Higher Education: A Challenge to Human Resource Managers." *CUPA Journal,* 1995, *46*(3), 23–27.

Murray, J. P., and Murray, J. I. "Job Satisfaction and the Propensity to Leave an Institution Among Two-Year College Division Chairpersons." 1998, 25(4), 45–59.

Near, J. P., and Sorcinelli, M. D. "Work and Life Away from Work: Predictors of Faculty Satisfaction." *Research in Higher Education,* 1986, *25,* 377–394.

Nobbe, J., and Manning, S. "Issues for Women in Student Affairs with Children." *NASPA Journal,* 1997, *34,* 101–111.

Reeves, M. E. "An Analysis of Job Satisfaction of Women Administrators in Higher Education." *Journal of the National Association for Deans, Administrators, and Counselors,* 1975, *38,* 132–135.

Reinhold, B. B. *Toxic Work: How to Overcome Stress, Overload, and Burnout and Revitalize Your Career.* New York: Dutton, 1996.

Reisser, L. J., and Zurfluh, L. A. "Female Administrators: Moving Up or Moving Out?" *Journal of the National Association for Deans, Administrators, and Counselors,* 1987, *50*(4), 22–29.

Rentz, A. L., and Associates. *Student Affairs Practice in Higher Education.* (2nd ed.) Springfield, Ill.: Thomas, 1996.

Rice, R. W., Near, J. P., and Hunt, R. G. "The Job-Satisfaction/Life-Satisfaction Relationship: A Review of Empirical Research." *Basic and Applied Social Psychology,* 1980, *1*(1), 37–64.

Richard, G. V. "The Effects of Stress, Strain and Coping on Male and Female Faculty at Differing Occupational Levels." Unpublished doctoral dissertation, University of Kansas, 1987.

Sagaria, M.A.D. *Head Counting, Hill Climbing, and Beyond: The Status and Future Directions for Research on Mid-Level Administrators' Careers.* San Antonio, Tex.: Association for the Study of Higher Education, 1986. (ED 268 891)

Schonwetter, D. J., Bond, S. L., and Perry, R. P. "Women Academic and Career Administrators' Role Perceptions and Occupational Satisfaction: Implications for Appointment and Professional Development." Paper presented at the American Educational Research Association, Atlanta, Apr. 1993.

Scott, N. A. "Chief Student Affairs Officers: Stressors and Strategies." *Journal of College Student Development,* 1992, *33*(2), 108–116.

Scott, N. A., and Spooner, S. "Women Administrators: Stressors and Strategies." *Journal of the National Association for Deans, Administrators, and Counselors,* 1989, *52*(2), 31–36.

Seldin, P. "Research Findings on Causes of Academic Stress." In P. Seldin (ed.), *Coping with Faculty Stress.* San Francisco: Jossey-Bass, 1987.

Skipper, T. L. "Stress Affects Student Affairs Professionals' Health." *ACU-I Bulletin,* 1992, *60*(2), 4–9.

Solomon, L. C., and Tierney, M. L. "Determinants of Job Satisfaction Among College Administrators." *Journal of Higher Education,* 1977, *68,* 412–431.

Steward, R. J., and others. "Women in Higher Education and Job Satisfaction: Does Interpersonal Style Matter?" *NASPA Journal,* 1995, *33,* 45–53.

Tait, M., Padgett, M. Y., and Baldwin, T. T. "Job and Life Satisfaction: A Reevaluation of the Strength of the Relationship and Gender Effects as a Function of the Date of Study." *Journal of Applied Psychology,* 1989, *74,* 501–507.

Tarver, D., Canada, R., and Lim, M. G. "The Relationship Between Job Satisfaction and Locus of Control Among College Student Affairs Administrators and Academic Administrators." *NASPA Journal,* 1999, *36*(2), 96–105.

Thoreson, R. W., Kardash, C. A., Leuthold, D. A., and Morrow, K. A. "Gender Differences in the Academic Career." *Research in Higher Education,* 1990, *31*(2), 193–209.

Villadsen, A. W., and Tack, M. W. "Combining Home and Career Responsibilities: The Methods Used by Women Executives in Higher Education." *Journal of the National Association for Deans, Administrators, and Counselors,* 1981, *4*(1), 20–25.

Volkwein, J. F., Malik, S. M., and Napierski-Prancl, M. "Administrative Satisfaction and the Regulatory Climate at Public Universities." *Research in Higher Education,* 1998, *39*(1), 43–63.

Ward, L. "Role Stress and Propensity to Leave Among New Student Affairs Professionals." *NASPA Journal,* 1995, *33,* 35–44.

Weishaar, M., Chiaravalli, K., and Jones, F. "Dual-Career Couples in Higher Education." *Journal of the National Association for Deans, Administrators, and Counselors,* 1984, *47*(4), 16–20.

Witt, S. L., and Lovrich, N. P. "Sources of Stress Among Faculty: Gender Differences." *Review of Higher Education,* 1988, *11*(3), 269–284.

Zurfluh, L. A., and Reisser, L. "A Comparison of Sources of Dissatisfaction Among Male and Female Administrators." Paper presented at the International Conference for Women in Higher Education, El Paso, Tex., Jan. 1990.

JANET E. ANDERSON *is joint director of student activities at the College of Saint Benedict and Saint John's University in Minnesota.*

FLORENCE GUIDO-DIBRITO *is associate professor in the College Student Personnel Administration Ph.D. program at the University of Northern Colorado.*

JEAN SCHOBER MORRELL *is dean of students at the University of Northern Colorado.*

INDEX

Academic medical centers (AMCs): changes due to financial presssures on, 39; described, 33; three primary missions, 34. *See also* Academic medicine faculty satisfaction

Academic medicine: cross-subsidization/clinical educator of, 34–35; faculty of, 33; growth of, 34; impact of managed care on, 35–36

Academic medicine faculty satisfaction: factors affecting, 37–40, 38*t*; models of, 36*f*–40; outcomes of faculty effort and, 37; outcomes potentially affected by, 37*t*; paradigm shift and, 34–36

Adams, G. A., 11

Adelmann, P. K., 102

Administrators. *See* Student affairs administrators

African American faculty, 60, 61, 63

Aisenberg, N., 21, 22

Allen, M. S., 87

AMCs. *See* Academic medical centers (AMCs)

American Federation of Teachers, 46

American Indian faculty, 62

Andersen, M. L., 29

Anderson, J. E., 99, 102, 103

Anderson, K. D., 39

Andrews, F. M., 102

Antonio, A. L., 58, 60, 63, 64

Antonnucci, T. C., 102

Aronowitz, S., 46, 49, 50

Asian Pacific American faculty, 59, 60

Association of American Medical Colleges (AAMC), 35

Association of American University Professors, 46

Astin, H. S., 23, 24, 28, 58, 60, 63

Austin, A., 99

Baldridge, V. J., 45, 47, 48, 49, 50

Baldwin, R. G., 10, 11

Baldwin, T. T., 103

Balkin, D. B., 49

Bassi, L. J., 87, 89

Bauer, K. W., 87, 97

Bedeian, A. G., 99

Bender, B. E., 100, 101, 106

Benjamin, E., 82

Bensimon, E. M., 23, 25, 26

Berwick, K. R., 105

Bickel, J., 38, 39

Bird, G. W., 103

Black, A. S., 60

Blackburn, R. T., 36, 37, 59

Blackhurst, A. E., 102, 106

Blackwell, J., 60

Blandin, J., 47

Block, S. D., 39

Bloland, P. A., 101

Bloom, A., 5

Blumenthal, D., 35, 37, 40

Boening, C., 68

Boice, R., 58, 73

Bond, S. L., 100

Boone, C. W., 100

Bowen, H., 69

Branch, W. T., Jr., 35

Brandt, J. E., 102, 106

Braskamp, L. A., 11

Brawer, F. B., 46, 47, 49

Brenenman, D. W., 84, 85

Brown, R. D., 104, 105

Brown, S. V., 60

Brown University study, 104

Bryson, M., 22

Bullers, S., 8

Burns, M. A., 106

Burrow, G. N., 34

Busenberg, B. E., 58

Calling: Essays on Teaching in the Mother Tongue (Griffin), 23

Cameron, K., 46

Campbell, E. W., 37, 39, 40

Campus multiculturalism perceptions, 93–94

Canada, R., 101

Capwell, D. F., 7

Carr, P. L., 39

Castro, C. R., 45, 55

Chamberlain, M. K., 21, 22

Chávez, R. C., 58, 61, 64

Chiaravalli, K., 104

Child care issues, 91

Chlinwiak, L., 22

Faculty satisfaction: in academic medicine, 33–40; community college faculty unions and, 45–54; of faculty of color, 57–65; importance of, 5–6; indicators for, 22; job satisfaction framework applied to, 10–12; sabbatical leave and, 73–74; of women faculty members, 21–30. *See also* Classified employee satisfaction
Faculty unions. *See* Community college faculty unions
Family-related changes: global job satisfaction by, 15*f*; as job satisfaction trigger, 11
Feminist Teaching in Theory and Practice: Situation Power and Knowledge in Poststructural Classrooms (Ropers-Huilman), 23
Ferrari, K., 12
Ferris, G. R., 95
Feuille, P., 47
Fields of Play: Constructing an Academic Life (Richardson), 23
Financial retrenchment, 88–89
Fink, L., 27
Finkel, S. K., 26
Finley, C. E., 49
Flint, C. B., 29
Foley, R., 39
Forde, L., 12
Fried, L. P., 37, 39
Friedman, E. G., 29
Frink, D. D., 92, 95
Furnham, A., 12

Gainen, J., 58
Gallagher, W. E., Jr., 8
Gallup Organization survey, 88
Gappa, J. M., 77, 79, 80, 81, 82, 83, 84, 85, 86
Garr, D. R., 39
Garza, H., 59, 60, 61
Gawel, J. E., 8
Gender differences: in administrator's job satisfaction, 100–101, 102; in institutional support, 39; in inter-role conflict, 103–104; in life satisfaction of administrators, 102. *See also* Women faculty satisfaction
Genel, M., 34, 35
Georgia State University's College of Arts and Sciences, 82
Gilligan, C., 21
Girard, C., 39

Glazer-Raymo, J., 22, 27
Glick, N. L., 100, 101, 106
Global life satisfaction, 15*f*–17*f*
Gomez-Mejia, L. R., 49
Good, C. V., 68, 69
Graf, L. A., 8, 47, 48
Green, M., 64
Greene, M., 27
Greenhaus, J. H., 99
Greer, D. S., 39
Greisler, H. P., 34, 35, 36, 39
Griffin, G. B., 21, 23, 24
Griffith, L. E., 39, 40
Griner, P. F., 35
Guadraz, G., 57
Guido-DiBrito, F., 99
Gumport, P., 26

Haeger, J. D., 80
Hagedorn, L. S., 5, 10, 12, 22, 24, 29, 57, 66, 91
Halcón, J. J., 61, 64
Hall, R. M., 29
Harding, S., 27
Harrigan, M. N., 11
Harrington, M., 21, 22
Harvey, W., 59, 60, 64
Heinig, S. J., 34, 35
Hemmasi, M., 8, 47, 48
Hensel, N., 5, 22, 106
Hersi, D. T., 106
Herzberg, F., 7, 8, 89
Higgins, C., 11
Hitchcock, M. A., 33, 43
Hobgood, W. P., 48, 49
Hochschild, A. R., 24
Holland, J. R., 5
Hollingsworth, S., 21
Hollins, E., 67, 68
Horowitz, H. L., 21
House, J., 93
Howard, J. L., 92, 95
Hudley, D. M., 33, 35
Hugick, L., 99, 100, 102
Hunt, R. G., 103
Hurrell, J. J., Jr., 87, 93, 94
Hutchins, R. M., 5
Hygienes, 7–8

Iannello, K. P., 107
Inglehart, J. K., 35, 36
Ingraham, M., 69
Inside American Education: The Decline, the Deception, the Dogmas (Sowell), 6

Back Issue/Subscription Order Form

Copy or detach and send to:
Jossey-Bass Publishers, 350 Sansome Street, San Francisco CA 94104-1342

Call or fax toll free!
Phone 888-378-2537 6AM-5PM PST; Fax 800-605-2665

Back issues: Please send me the following issues at $23 each
                (Important: please include series initials and issue number, such as IR90)

1. IR _____

_____

_____

$ _____ Total for single issues

$ _____ Shipping charges (for single issues ***only;*** subscriptions are exempt
              from shipping charges): Up to $30, add $5^{50} • $30^{01}–$50, add $6^{50}
              $50^{01}–$75, add $8 • $75^{01}–$100, add $10 • $100^{01}–$150, add $12
              Over $150, call for shipping charge

Subscriptions   Please ❑ start   ❑ renew my subscription to *New Directions for
                Institutional Research* for the year _____ at the following rate:

                U.S.   ❑ Individual $56   ❑ Institutional $99
                Canada: ❑ Individual $81   ❑ Institutional $124
                All Others: ❑ Individual $86   ❑ Institutional $129
                NOTE: Subscriptions are quarterly, and are for the calendar year only.
                Subscriptions begin with the Spring issue of the year indicated above.

$ _____ Total single issues and subscriptions (Add appropriate sales tax
              for your state for single issue orders. No sales tax for U.S. subscriptions.
              Canadian residents, add GST for subscriptions and single issues.)

❑ Payment enclosed (U.S. check or money order only)

❑ VISA, MC, AmEx, Discover Card #_____ Exp. date_____

Signature _____ Day phone _____

❑ Bill me (U.S. institutional orders only. Purchase order required)

Purchase order #_____

Federal Tax ID 135593032   GST 89102-8052

Name _____

Address _____

_____

Phone_____ E-mail _____

For more information about Jossey-Bass Publishers, visit our Web site at:
www.josseybass.com   **PRIORITY CODE = ND1**

OTHER TITLES AVAILABLE IN THE
NEW DIRECTIONS FOR INSTITUTIONAL RESEARCH SERIES
J. Fredericks Volkwein, Editor-in-Chief